MW00862145

ESSENTIAL
ART AS
THERAPY
FOR YOUTH

Dearest Drew

Thank you for being a bright Light in this world

I hope you enjoy the book with your girls ♡.

♡ -Cath
Guzman

ESSENTIAL ART AS THERAPY FOR YOUTH

Creative Ways to Express BIG Emotions

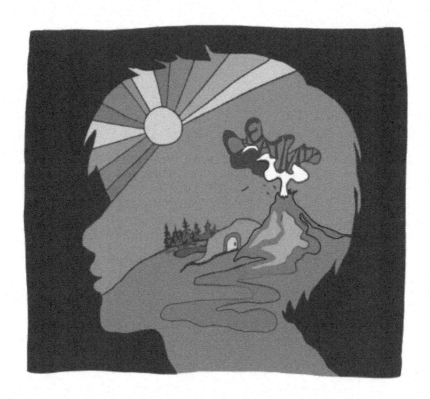

LEAH GUZMAN, ATR-BC

Copyrighted Material

Essential Art As Therapy For Youth:
Creative Ways to Express BIG Emotions

Copyright © 2024 by Leah Guzman Studio. All Rights Reserved.

No part of this publication may be reproduced, stored in a retrieval system or transmitted, in any form or by any means—electronic, mechanical, photocopying, recording, or otherwise—without prior written permission from the publisher, except for the inclusion of brief quotations in a review.

For information about this title, contact the publisher:

Leah Guzman
www.leahguzman.com
www.leahguzmanstudio.com

ISBNs:
978-1-7379202-2-9 (softcover)
978-1-7379202-3-6 (eBook)

Printed in the United States of America

Cover art and interior art work created by Leah Guzman

Nonfiction, Self-Help, Art Therapy, stress relief for children and adolescents, coping skills, emotional regulation, art making, mixed media, Art Techniques, children psychology, kids feelings, therapy for kids, Psychology and Counseling, Mental Health, Medical Psychology, Crafts, Hobbies and Home Arts, Photography, Alternative Medicine, Art Therapy, and Relaxation Medicine

This book is dedicated to all the amazing young people I worked with in my career as an art therapist. I also dedicate the book to the next generation of art therapists, providing services in schools around the world, teaching our youth empathy and coping tools to manage big emotions.

Contents

Chapter 1

Introduction

Scan for video

My intention for writing this book is based on the desire to let you know how powerful art can be in healing and teaching children. Learning how to manage our emotions isn't one of the main priorities taught in school. Managing emotions is a key component to excelling at school and learning. It's my goal to bring art as therapy to youth, so they can have a space to express themselves creatively. A space to explore their feelings and process their emotions. My big dream is to have art therapy services in all schools to teach empathy and coping skills to manage big emotions.

I'm Leah Guzman, a board-certified art therapist and practicing artist with more than 20 years of experience. I specialize in helping young people find healthy ways to express themselves, particularly those facing challenges. Throughout my career, primarily working with at-risk students in public schools, I've discovered that building strong connections is key to unlocking their potential.

Children blossom when they're allowed to explore and express themselves through play, especially artistic play. This playful learning not only strengthens their emotional vocabulary but also lays the groundwork for future success, as research by Dr. Horacio Sanchez suggests. His work highlights three key principles that foster emotional regulation in children: a sense of accomplishment, consistent routines, and strong connections.

Unlocking success starts with small achievements, like completing the projects in this book. The feel-good hormone dopamine is released when we complete tasks. Consistency, the second key principle, comes from carving out time and space for your mental well-being. Routines provide predictability and comfort, knowing what to expect each day. These exercises can be done after school or incorporated into a weekly routine. Mark your calendar now to schedule your practice sessions! Finally, connection, the third principle, thrives on positive interactions. Simple gestures like a warm smile and showing genuine interest in someone's hobbies can build strong connections, which is the foundation of this book.

What is the difference between art therapy and art as therapy?

If you are teaching or providing services to a youth with behavioral concerns to the extent that it's interrupting their daily functioning (e.g., acting-out behaviors or isolation), then it's important to consult a trained professional to provide individual art therapy sessions. Art therapy will provide a safe space to process behavioral and emotional concerns with clinical theoretical practices. Trained art therapists can equip young people facing past traumas or disruptive behavior with the tools they need to navigate challenges and achieve success, one brushstroke at a time.

This book isn't therapy in the traditional sense, even though I'm a certified art therapist. It's art *as* therapy.

It provides a fun, creative space for children to express their emotions, manage big feelings, and bond with you. As you explore the exercises together, you might even discover a little healing for yourself!

My mission is to spark hope in young minds, not just through words but also through the transformative power of art. I envision safe spaces where children can:

+ Find inner calm: Breathe deeply, let go of anxieties, and immerse themselves in the present moment.
+ Decrease anxiety: Express their emotions freely through art, allowing worries to take form and fade away.
+ Learn to regulate their nervous system: Develop healthy coping mechanisms and build resilience through creative exploration.

There's no "right" or "wrong" in art. Judgment has no place here. The magic lies in unleashing your inner artist, embracing individuality, and letting your emotions flow onto the canvas, paper, or whatever medium speaks to you.

Feel free to explore. Experiment. Get messy. Every stroke, every splash of color, tells a story. And in that story lies the potential for healing, growth, and, most importantly, hope.

A QR code is provided that links you to a pre-recorded video of the lessons, so that we can create together. This way, you can follow along with me.

The exercises in each chapter are a deep dive of various ways you can explore a particular feeling. I would recommend doing the exercises within the chapter you choose in order, because they build skills. The exercises can be done once or twice a week to support emotional well-being. You can post your art created from this book in the private Facebook group, Creative Soul Online Retreat.

Prepare to be empowered! The number 8, symbolizing transformation and insight, is woven throughout this experience. Explore 8 chapters packed with 88 exercises designed to unlock your potential. Look for hidden keys (my personal logo) in the drawings; finding them represents unlocking something special within yourself. How many can you discover?

I recommend the drawing exercises be done in a journal. Journals are a safe container to hold emotions. These exercises can be done individually or in a classroom setting. This book is filled with exercises that include drawing, painting, collage-making, sculpture, and journaling to address emotions and life's challenges. Below is a list of all materials used in this book. You can order your own kit to get started at www.leahguzmanstudio.com.

TIP: For a better viewing experience, you can watch the lesson videos on a larger screen by visiting www.arthealsyouth.com/videolessons from your computer.

You'll find a list of all the chapters there, and with just one click, you can enjoy them on your laptop, tablet, or desktop.

Materials:

Scan for video

+ Art journal (8"x10" or 5"x 7")
+ Pens
+ Color pencils

- Markers
- Oil crayons
- Crayons
- Acrylic paint
- Brushes
- Water container
- Scissors
- Glue stick
- Hot-glue gun and sticks
- Magazines, craft paper for collage
- Camera for selfies
- Printer to print feeling selfies
- Blue painter's tape
- Newspaper
- Plaster rigid wrap
- Mentos candy/diet soda
- Self-drying drying clay
- Model Magic
- Tin foil
- Black Sharpee marker
- Plastic wrap
- Clay-sculpting tools
- Felt squares
- Polyester stuffing
- Needle, thread, and pins
- Blow dryer or hot-air gun
- Drop cloth
- Stickers
- Chalk
- Projector
- Gloves
- Butcher paper

Chapter 2

Unlocking Confidence:
A Journey of Self-Discovery

Building confidence begins with a profound understanding of yourself. This journey starts by identifying your **strengths**—those core abilities that form the foundation of your sense of worth. Through introspection and exploration, you'll delve into the vital relationships and activities that shape your life, revealing aspects of yourself you may not have fully recognized.

Scan for video

2-1 Personalize Your Journal Painting

Benefit: Establishing a personal space where you can express yourself creatively

Exercise Time: 30 minutes

Ages: Elementary 5+, middle, and high school

Materials:
- Acrylic paint
- Pencil
- Art journal
- Brushes
- Paint markers
- Collage materials (print images from the internet or use magazines)
- Scissors
- Glue

Explanation:

Your art journal is more than just a book; it's a canvas for your emotions, a companion on your creative journey, and a silent friend whenever you need it. Choose an image that represents you to personalize your journal. This can be one of your favorite things that you like to do. The most important thing is to make the journal an extension of your unique self. Use materials that speak to you, whether it's paint, pencil, or glitter!

Steps:
1. Choose an image to represent you from a magazine or printed from the internet.
2. Pick colors for the background, and apply to cover of the journal.
3. Attach your image to the cover of journal with glue.
4. Add details with paint markers, acrylic paint, or stickers.

Questions for Discussion:
1. Tell me more about your cover design.
2. This journal is a place to create art and share ideas. What ideas do you have to put into it?
3. Keep your journal in a safe space. Will you keep it in your backpack, desk, or bedside? Will you have an adult hold it for you?

Scan for video

2-2   Strength Shield Drawing

Benefit: Builds strengths and confidence

Exercise Time: 45 minutes

☛ **Ages:** Elementary 5+, middle, and high school

Materials:
☛ Art journal

☛ Assorted drawing media (markers, oil crayons, colored pencils)

Explanation:
Everyone possesses unique strengths, be it in a specific sport, activity, or intrinsic character traits. Discovering these strengths allows you to identify aspects of yourself that spark pride and fulfillment. This self-awareness empowers you to build resilience when faced with life's challenges. Even if you're currently struggling, recognizing your inherent strengths provides a foundation for growth and perseverance.

Steps:
1. Draw a shield.
2. Write name on the top of the shield.
3. Divide shield into four parts.
4. Draw and name a strength in each section.
5. Examples:
   a. Sports
   b. Hobbies
   c. Activities
   d. Personality characteristics: outgoing, kind, caring, thoughtful
6. Color in the shield.
7. Hang it up.

Questions for Discussion:
1. Tell me about your strengths.
2. How can your strengths help you when times are challenging?
3. Can you give me an example of when you would use one of your strengths if you felt a big emotion? (e.g., sadness, grief) You can draw a picture.

Scan for video

2-3   Magical Treehouse Painting

Benefit: Use your imagination to create your own place of escape

Exercise Time: 30 minutes

Ages: Elementary 5+, middle, and high school

Materials:
- Art journal
- Markers
- Oil crayons
- Watercolors
- Brushes
- Water container

Explanation:
Imagine a magical treehouse, your own personal sanctuary nestled amongst the trees and leaves. Will it be a lofty perch, high in the branches, offering sweeping views of the world below? Or perhaps a cozy haven tucked away in the shrubs, a hidden fort waiting to be explored. Let your creativity flow as you design your dream hideaway.

Steps:
1. Draw out your tree.
2. Add your treehouse (base, walls, windows, roof).
3. You can draw it open to show what you have inside or keep it closed.
4. Add a way to get into your house (ladder, slide, wooden steps).
5. Add all the items that you would want to bring with you.
6. Draw yourself there.
7. Color in with watercolors.

Questions for Discussion:
1. Tell me all about your house.
2. Is this a place you would visit often?
3. Who would you like to invite to your treehouse?
4. What would you do there, and what would you bring with you?

Scan for video

2-4   Name Game Drawing

Benefit: Improves self-awareness and increases personal strengths

Exercise Time: 30 minutes

Ages: Elementary 5+, middle, and high school

Materials:
- Art journal
- Assorted drawing media (markers, oil crayon, colored pencils)

Explanation:
The "name game" is where each letter of your name becomes a starting point to describe yourself. It's also a wonderful way for you to discover and celebrate your positive qualities.

Steps:
1. Use block letters to write your name in the journal vertically.
2. Find strength words for each of the letters in your name.
3. Use the list of words provided in the back of the book, create your own, or look on the internet for inspiration. Refer to strength list on page 194.
4. Write the strength word next to each letter of your name.

Questions for Discussion:
1. Is there one word that you really like to describe yourself?
2. Would you like to be called by your strength name?
3. How would you like to be known by others?

Lovely

Excited

Awesome

Hopeful

Scan for video

2-5　All About You Painting

Benefit: Enhances self-awareness, boosts confidence, and improves emotional processing

Exercise Time: 1.5 hours (two meetings of 45 minutes each)

Ages: Elementary 5+, middle, and high school

Materials:
- 12"x18" watercolor paper
- Black Sharpee Marker
- Watercolor
- Brushes
- Water container

- Pencil
- Markers
- Black acrylic paint
- Cell phone or flashlight
- Blue painter's tape

Explanation:

Imagine creating a window into your world, a unique portrait that reveals what truly matters to you. This is your chance to share your passions, interests, and everything that makes you amazing. This isn't just about copying what you see but rather about expressing it through your own creative vision. Think of it as a special X-ray that captures the essence of your imagination and allows others to connect with you on a deeper level.

Steps:
1. Attach paper to wall with painter's tape.
2. Place projector or light from phone 3 feet away from the wall.
3. Trace the silhouette from your head to your shoulders.
4. On the inside of the silhouette, draw out your favorite things, such as:
   - Food
   - Place
   - Objects
   - People important to you
   - Animal
   - Book characters or superheroes
   - Activities and games
5. Outline the drawings inside of the profile with black marker.
6. Paint the outside of the profile black.
7. Color in with colored markers.
8. Fill in spaces with watercolor paint.

Questions for Discussion:
1. What is your favorite part of this piece?
2. Who and what are important to you?
3. If you were a color, what color would you be?

Scan for video

2-6   Strength Coil Pot Sculpture

Benefit: Identifying strengths to help you blossom

Exercise Time: 30 minutes

Ages: Elementary 5+, middle, and high school

Materials:
- Model magic: various colors
- Art journal
- Pencil

Explanation:
Imagine a funky-looking vase, each vibrant coil representing a unique strength that resides within you. This is an organic sculpture, and it is not about perfection. It may have lots of twists and bends. As you look upon your creation, remember that your strengths and values are woven within each coil.

Steps:
1. Identify one of your strengths or values (refer to lists at the back of the book, p. 194).
2. Pick a color to represent your strength.
3. Create a ball, and flatten it to make a circle shape for the base.
4. Roll the model magic into a coil.
5. Place the coil on top of the flattened base.
6. Continue making coils and placing them on top of each other to make the vase taller.
7. Make new colors by mixing 2 colors of model magic together.
8. List each strength and the color in your journal.
9. Let the coil pot dry overnight to become firm.

Question for Discussion:
1. Which color coil do you like most?
2. Which is your favorite strength?
3. How would you like to use the coil pot?

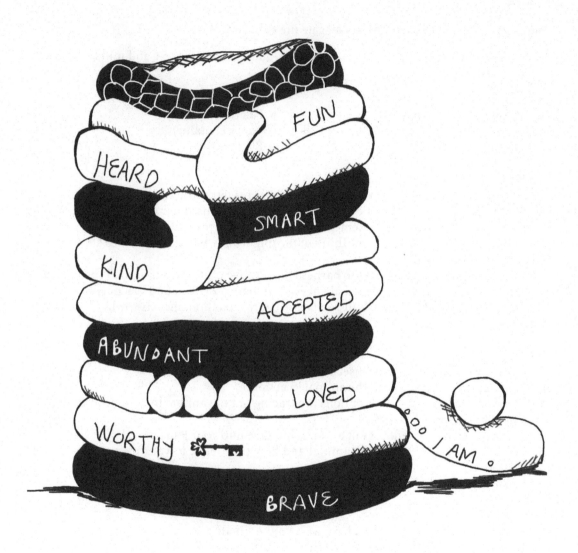

Scan for video

2-7   Powerful Animal Painting

Benefit: Channeling strengths to navigate life's challenges

Exercise Time: 45 minutes   **Ages:** Elementary 5+ and middle school

Materials:
- Art journal: or print animal
- Printer paper for tracing
- Assorted drawing media (markers, colored pencils, gel pens)
- Acrylic Paint
- Palette
- Water container
- Brushes

Explanation:

Imagine yourself venturing into a magical world where your spirit takes the form of an animal. Each creature in this world embodies a specific set of strengths and unique challenges, offering valuable lessons along the way. Remember, size isn't everything. Even the smallest creatures hold immense power within them. Think of the mighty ant, with its incredible ability to carry 40 times its own weight.

Now, the opportunity is yours to harness the positive traits of your animal spirit. Channel its strengths as you navigate life's challenges, overcome obstacles, and reach new heights. So, which animal will you choose? Will you be the courageous lion, the wise owl, or, perhaps, the transformational butterfly?

Steps:
1. Choose a favorite animal or insect.
2. Look up an image online of the animal in action.
3. Draw out the animal. Other options are tracing out the animal by using the computer as a light box or print.
4. If you traced or printed, cut out animal, and glue into your journal.
5. Write out the strengths of the animal and how they relate to your own strengths in the journal.
6. Color the animal and its environment.

Questions for Discussion:
1. How many similarities do you have with your animal?
2. Do you have more than one animal that you can relate to?
3. What does your animal need in its environment to thrive?

Scan for video

2-8   Ripples of Positivity Painting

Benefit: Learning how to address negative comments

Exercise Time: 30 minutes

Ages: Elementary 5+, middle, and high school

Materials:
- Art journal
- Assorted drawing materials (markers, oil crayons, colored pencils)
- Acrylic Paint
- Brushes
- Palette
- Water Container

Explanation:

We've all been there—someone says something negative about us, and it sticks in our minds. It can take up to 14 positive statements to counteract the impact of just one negative one. Here's the key: We can create our own words and images to empower ourselves to rise above the negativity.

Steps:
1. What is a negative comment that someone has said about you?
2. Explore this comment with the youth.
3. Brainstorm positive words that validate the youth.
4. Create a drawing representing this validation.
5. Write "I AM" with the positive word in bubble letters.
6. Trace around the words 8 times to create ripples.
7. Paint in the ripples.

Questions for Discussion:
1. When was the last time you complimented someone?
2. When was the last time you received a compliment?

Scan for video

2-9   Superhero Sculpture

Benefit: Assists in identifying strengths in others and in oneself

Exercise Time: 45 minutes   **Ages:** Elementary 5+, and middle school

Materials:
- Tin foil (3 sheets)
- Hot glue
- Felt
- Rigid wrap
- Acrylic paint
- Brushes
- Palette

Explanation:

Do you ever dream of saving the day with incredible superpowers? Imagine your favorite superhero: how do they stand tall and proud? Are they soaring through the sky, ready to blast off with laser eyes, or perhaps offering a comforting embrace? Use tin foil to mold your hero's pose, whether it's arms raised in victory, wings outstretched, or ready to give a big hug. To make your hero even stronger, we'll add a special touch: a layer of rigid wrap. This will give your creation extra durability and make it ready for any adventure. Remember, every superhero has unique strengths, just like you. Through this exercise, we're not just creating a cool figurine but also celebrating the amazing qualities within ourselves.

Steps:
1. Take 3 large sheets of tin foil.
2. Roll each sheet into a long stick.
3. Bend one stick to make the body with a head.
4. Stick twist around the body to make arms.
5. Bend the third stick around body to make legs.
6. Pose the figure.
7. Dip the rigid wrap in the water, and layer on figure.
8. Cover the entire figure.
9. Once the figure is covered, allow it to dry for 10 minutes.
10. Paint the rigid wrap.
11. Attach felt for clothes.

Questions for Discussion:
1. What strengths does your superhero have?
2. If you could have superhero strengths, what would you want (invisible, fly, really strong, time travel, etc.)?
3. What are the strengths you have right now?

Scan for video

2-10 Strength Stack Drawing

Benefit: Builds confidence and self-esteem

Exercise Time: 45 minutes

Ages: Elementary 5+, middle, high school

Materials:
- Refer to Strength List in back of book
- Sharpee marker
- Art journal
- Assorted drawing media (markers, colored pencils, gel pens)

Explanation:
Studies have shown that learners with higher confidence are more willing to learn, challenge themselves, and have better resilience in challenging times. Confidence is the number-one predictor of academic achievement. Let's continue the journey of building confidence. Recognize your strengths to find courage through challenging times.

Steps:
1. Create an outline of head.
2. Pick out 8 strengths from the list on page 194.
3. Write out the words inside the profile of the head.
4. Use assorted drawing media to design it.

Questions for Discussion:
1. What is your favorite part of you?
2. What colors express your true essence?

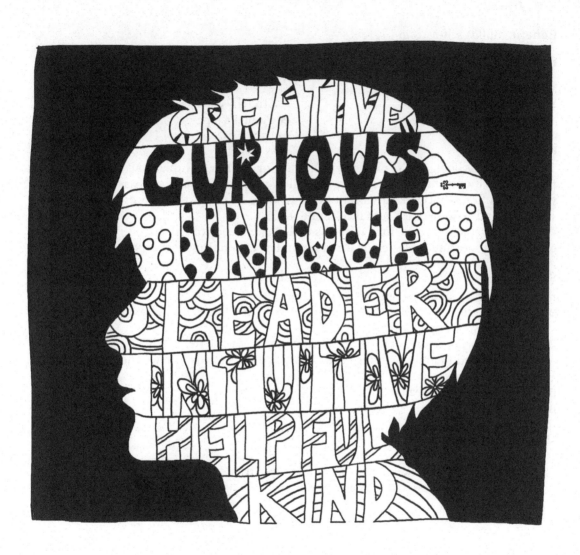

Scan for video

2-11   Strength Bracelets

Benefit: Builds self-esteem

Exercise Time: 30 minutes

Ages: Elementary 5+, middle, high school

Materials:
- Color beads
- Letter beads
- Stretchy cord
- Painter's tape

Explanation:

Throughout this book, you've explored your amazing qualities. Think about the qualities that resonate most with you. Perhaps you're incredibly resilient, like a strong elastic cord. Maybe you're full of creativity, like a vibrant bead. Choose elements that represent your unique strengths, and create a bracelet that celebrates them.

Don't forget to make one for a friend as well. Share the joy of self-discovery, and empower each other by wearing these personalized reminders of your inner superpowers.

Steps:

1. Cut the string, and tape one side to the table.
2. Find the letters of the strength words you would like to use for the bracelet. Refer to the strength list on page 194.
3. Add color beads to half of the bracelet, and then add the letter beads.
4. You will need to add the letter beads in spelled backwards to have the word come out spelled correctly.
5. Add the rest of the beads.
6. Tie a knot at the end.

Questions for Discussion:

1. What are your strengths?
2. Who else would you like to make a bracelet for: a friend, teacher, or parent?

Scan for video

2-12 Goal Getter Drawing

Benefit: Creates self-awareness, promotes positive thinking, and builds problem-solving skills

Exercise Time: 45 minutes   **Ages:** Elementary 8+, middle, high school

Materials:
- Art journal
- Assorted drawing media (markers, oil crayons, colored pencils)

Explanation:
Deep down, we all have desires, aspirations, and goals we want to achieve. This is your chance to claim what you truly want and take the first steps toward making it happen.

Do you dream of excelling in your studies? Perhaps you're looking forward to making new friends or new learning opportunities at school. The key lies in identifying the steppingstones that will lead you to your destination. What actions can you take, big or small, to move closer to your goal? Remember, even the grandest journeys begin with a single step.

Steps:
1. Identify what you really want.
2. Draw out what you want on one side of your journal.
3. Discuss the steps needed to get there.
4. Draw out the steps to get goal as steppingstones.
5. Color in the image.

Questions for Discussion:
1. What is the first step you can take today?
2. Who else can help you reach your goal?
3. Track your progress, and reward yourself (use an agenda or create a chart).

Scan for video

2-13 Dream Team Drawing

Benefit: Creating a support system to build resilience

Exercise Time: 30 minutes

Ages: Elementary 5+, middle, and high school

Materials:
- Art journal
- Assorted drawing materials (markers, oil crayons, colored pencils)

Explanation:
Imagine yourself building a strong and supportive community of people, a team you can rely on through thick and thin. Recognize the importance of having these connections in your life.

Think about the people who make you feel safe, loved, and understood. It could be a family member, a friend, a teacher, or even someone you haven't met yet. These are the individuals you look up to, trust, and feel comfortable seeking help from when you need it.

Remember, building this support system takes time and effort. If you haven't yet identified someone who fulfills these roles, consider opening yourself up to new connections and fostering positive relationships. Everyone needs a team, and you are worthy of building one that empowers and supports your journey.

Steps:
1. Draw yourself in the middle of the page.
2. Draw out the people in your life who are important to you and part of your community.
3. Connect each member to you.
4. Color the image.
5. Identify each person by name.

Questions for Discussion:
1. Can you tell me more about this person?
2. What are some memories you've had with them?
3. What do you like about them?

Scan for video

2-14 Letter to My Future Self Drawing

Benefit: Visualizing the future for self-determination and goal setting

Exercise Time: 45 minutes

Ages: Elementary 8+, middle, and high school

Materials:
- Art journal
- Assorted drawing materials (markers, oil crayons, colored pencils)

Explanation:

As kids, we often dream of exciting careers and amazing experiences. Close your eyes, and envision yourself in the future. What kind of adventures do you want to have? What kind of job do you want to have in the future? What contributions do you want to make to the world? Use your imagination, and play with the idea of what you would like to do (e.g., write a book, become a chef, or help animals).

Remember, your dreams can evolve and transform over time. Embrace the journey of self-discovery, and keep an open mind to new paths that may unfold.

Steps:
1. Write a letter to your future self, as if you were writing to a best friend.
2. Start your letter with "Dear (your name)."
3. What do you want to say to your future self?
4. What words of encouragement can you give yourself?
5. Sign your letter, and date it.
6. Draw your future self.

Questions for Discussion:
1. Read your letter out loud.
2. Keep it in a safe place, or save this art journal to enjoy at a later date.

DEAR _____ ,

_____

_____

_____

_____

_____

_____

_____

_____

_____

_____

♥

_____

Scan for video

2-15 Best Me Selfie Mixed Media Collage

Benefit: Improves self-awareness, emotion regulation, and coping skills

Exercise Time: 45 minutes

Ages: Elementary 5+, middle, and high school

Materials:
- Art journal
- Printed picture of self (full-body or portrait)
- Assorted drawing media (markers, oil crayons, colored pencils)
- Acrylic paint
- Stickers
- Glue stick
- Scissors

Explanation:

Invest in yourself. Get a good night's sleep, nourish your body with healthy food, move your body regularly, get your homework done, and make time to enjoy nature. In this collage, you will take a picture of yourself, and then you will incorporate all the things that you enjoy participating in that make you feel good.

Steps:
1. Take a picture of yourself with an expression of feeling your best.
2. Print image (black-and-white image works).
3. Cut out your image.
4. Glue to journal.
5. Add lines, shapes, and colors to your portrait, representing your best self.
6. You can add objects, activities, words, and symbols, too.

Questions for Discussion:
1. When was the last time you felt your best?
2. Where were you?
3. What happened?
4. What are things that you do to feel your best?

Scan for video

2-16 Best Me Feeling Feltie Plushie

Benefit: Increases awareness of feelings and develops coping skills

Exercise Time: 45 minutes

Ages: Elementary and middle school

Materials:
- Felt squares
- Pillow stuffing
- Needle and thread (or hot glue)
- Pins
- Paper
- Scissors
- Markers

Explanation:

Imagine you have a special friend who embodies all your strengths and qualities. This friend is about to be brought to life as a cuddly plushie. In this activity, you'll design a plushie that reflects your unique personality and maybe even some fantastical abilities. Think about the traits that make you special. Do you have a mischievous streak? Perhaps your plushie has mismatched socks or a playful wink. Are you known for your kindness? Maybe your plushie has a big, warm huggable heart.

Steps:
1. Draw the shape of your plushie in your journal.
2. Add details to form your character.
3. Trace out the shape onto paper to use as a template.
4. Place felt under template, and use pins to hold in place.
5. Cut out felt for the top and bottom of plushie.
6. Start by sewing the facial features (eyes, ears, clothing, horns, tail, etc.) first, attaching them with pins.
7. Next, sew together the two main body pieces. Hot glue can also be used.
8. Leave small opening space to fill with stuffing.
9. Finish sewing up body.

Questions for Discussion:
1. What is your favorite part of your plushie?
2. When was the last time you felt your best?

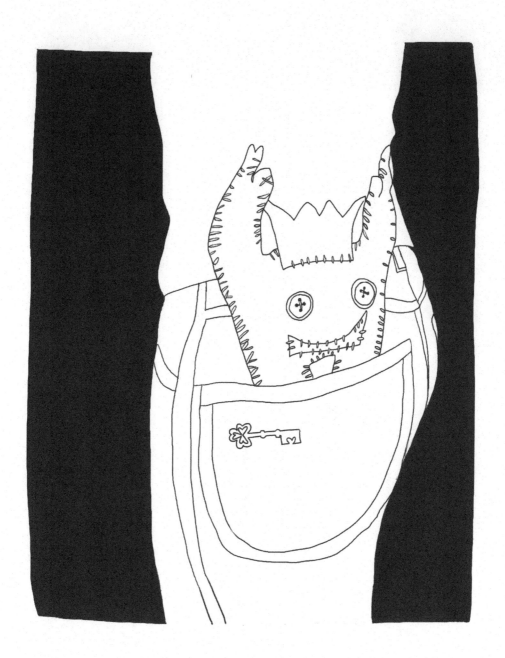

Chapter 3

Mastering Emotions

Regulating emotions and crafting self-care practices are like planting the seeds of a vibrant inner garden. By tending to your emotional landscape, you cultivate resilience, joy, and a deep sense of well-being. You will learn ways to master emotions. Self-care practices become essential tools in nurturing this belief, creating a safe space for your emotions to flourish. By cultivating supportive environments, you build a "container" that holds you up, allowing you to embrace your strengths and shine.

Scan for video

3-1 Feeling Scale Drawing

Benefit: Improves emotional regulation and self-reflection

Exercise Time: 2 minutes   **Ages:** Elementary 5+, middle, high school

Materials:
- Visual Rating Scale image
- Art journal
- Assorted drawing media (markers, oil crayons, colored pencils)

Explanation:
This exercise is designed to help you develop a powerful habit: daily emotional check-ins. It's a simple practice with significant benefits, allowing you to gain awareness of your emotions and how they fluctuate throughout the day.

The inspiration for this exercise comes from an art teacher who implemented a clever strategy in her classroom. During attendance, students wouldn't just say "present," but also share a number (1–5), indicating their current emotional state. This allowed the teacher to identify students who might need additional support and connect them with resources like the school counselor or art therapist. You can use this as a daily check-in, or on a weekly basis to check in with feelings.

Steps:
1. Make your own chart for the week in your art journal.
2. Choose your feeling on the visual chart from the feeling list on page 196.
3. 1 = feeling great; 2 = feeling okay; 3 = low energy; 4 = feeling sad; 5 = I need help

Questions for Discussion:
1. You can use this to monitor your own feelings throughout the week.
2. Who do you go to when you need help?

LEVEL	PERSON · PLACE · THING	MAKES ME FEEL
5		I NEED HELP
4		UPSET
3		LOW ENERGY
2		OKAY
1		AWESOME

Scan for video

3-2 Visual Check-In Drawing

Benefit: Identifies feelings to gain mastery over emotions

Exercise Time: 5–10 minutes

Ages: Elementary 8+, middle, and high school

Materials:
- Art journal
- Assorted drawing media (markers, oil crayons, colored pencils)

Explanation:

Use art media to explore and express your feelings visually. This involves expressing your emotions through lines, shapes, and colors.

Imagine your current emotion as a drawing. Are you feeling happy, sad, or angry? Try to capture this emotion as a drawing. Is this drawing sharp and jagged, like anger, or perhaps flowing and gentle, like calmness? What kind of lines or texture would you like to use? What colors would capture its essence? Is it the vibrant red of passion or the soothing blue of tranquility?

By translating your emotions into art, you gain a deeper understanding of yourself and your inner world. This visual representation can be a powerful tool for processing emotions, identifying triggers, and developing healthy coping mechanisms.

Steps:
1. Draw a large circle in your art journal.
2. Choose lines, shapes, and colors to represent how you feel. Refer to feeling chart on page 196.
3. Fill in the circle with color and texture.
4. Name your drawing.

Questions for Discussion:
1. Challenge: Can you practice a check-in drawing daily for a week?
2. What did you learn about yourself and your art?
3. Did any symbols come up for you? Are they important to you?

Scan for video

3-3 Feeling Flower Painting

Benefit: Identifies feelings to gain mastery over emotions

Exercise Time: 30 minutes

Ages: Elementary 5+, middle, and high school

Materials:
- Art journal
- Watercolor
- Pencil
- Refer to Feeling List in the back of the book

Explanation:

Have you ever felt overwhelmed by a wave of emotion? It can be difficult to navigate our feelings, especially when they seem to take control. But there's a powerful strategy to help you gain a sense of mastery: giving your emotions a name and a color.

This approach is based on the idea that acknowledging and labeling our emotions is the first step toward managing them effectively. By giving your emotions a name, you bring them into conscious awareness, allowing you to better understand their cause and potential impact.

The color association adds another layer of personal meaning. Colors evoke different feelings for each individual. For instance, while blue might symbolize calmness and peace for some, it could represent sadness for others. Choose colors that resonate with your own unique experiences.

Steps:
1. Draw a circle.
2. Divide the circle into 8.
3. Choose a feeling, and match it to a color.
4. Write the feeling word on top of the triangle shape.
5. Use lines and shapes to fill in the piece.
6. Repeat this process for 8 total emotions.
7. Add another layer of petals to your flower, and explore new words to describe those emotions.

Questions for Discussion:
1. Which emotion did you choose to do first?
2. Which new words did you choose to write in the second row of petals?
3. Which emotion do you feel most often?
4. Reflect on a time that these emotions have come up in your daily life.

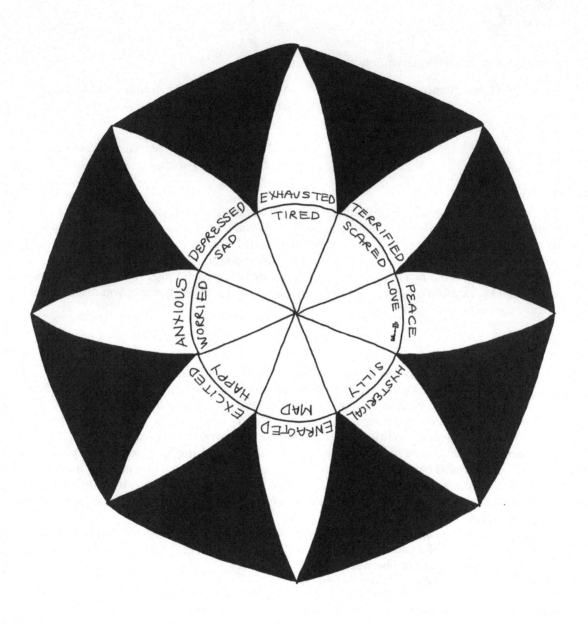

Scan for video

3-4 Grounding Hand Drawing

Benefit: Regulate your nervous system to reduce stress

Exercise Time: 30 minutes

Ages: Elementary 5+, middle, and high school

Materials:
- Art journal
- Pencil
- Assorted drawing materials: markers, gel pens, colored pencils

Explanation:

Life can throw curveballs, leaving us feeling overwhelmed and disoriented. During these times, it's crucial to have tools at your disposal to help you regain your sense of calm and being grounded. The "grounding hand" technique is a powerful strategy that utilizes your five senses to bring you back to the present moment and promote relaxation.

Imagine your hand as a gateway to your inner sanctuary. Each finger represents a specific sense, and by focusing on positive experiences associated with each sense, you can actively engage your entire being in the process of self-soothing.

Steps:
1. Use the pencil to trace your hand.
2. For each finger, identify one thing that calms you and relates to one of your senses.
3. **Sight:** Start with the thumb, and draw out an image that calms you related to sight. For example, imagine a visually calming scene, like a peaceful sunset or a field of flowers.
   Sound: Next, draw a soothing sound on your pointer finger. Think of a soothing sound, such as calming music, gentle waves breaking on the shore, or the rain.
   Smell: On your middle finger draw out a smell that is calming for you. Recall a pleasant aroma, like freshly baked cookies, lavender essential oil, or the scent of pine trees in a forest.
   Taste: On your ring finger, draw out a calming thing you can taste. Savor the memory of a delicious and comforting taste, like your favorite dessert, a warm cup of hot cocoa, or a piece of fresh fruit.
   Touch: Lastly, on your pinky finger, draw out something you can touch for calmness. Focus on the sensation of a comforting touch, such as a soft blanket, a hug from a loved one, a pet, or the feeling of sand between your toes.
4. Color in your hand with the items you chose.

Questions for Discussion:
1. When do you feel that you might need to use the grounding-hand items?
2. You can gather these items for your self-care kit.

Scan for video

3-5 Self-Care Kits Mixed Media

Benefit: Utilize your senses to reduce stress and regulate nervous system

Exercise Time: 30 minutes

Ages: Elementary 5+, middle, high school

Materials:
- Art journal
- Assorted drawing materials (gel pens, pencil, markers)
- Pencil Pouch
- Stickers
- Personal Photo
- Feeling Feltie Plushie
- Essential Oil
- Rubbing Stone
- Snack

Explanation:

Imagine having a personal toolbox filled with treasures that can help you navigate big emotions and find moments of peace. That's the essence of a self-care kit. The idea is to gather items that bring you comfort and joy, allowing you to soothe yourself during challenging times. Think of it as a portable hug, ready to offer support whenever you need it most.

Steps:

1. **Identify your calming tools:** What activities or items help you feel centered and relaxed? Do you find solace in creative expression through drawing or journaling? Perhaps a feeling feltie plushie or a favorite childhood toy brings back comforting memories. Maybe calming scents like lavender or chamomile do the trick.
2. **Gather your treasures:** Once you've identified your personal calming tools, it's time to gather them together and put them into a pouch.
3. **Make it accessible:** Keep your self-care kit in a convenient location, like your backpack you can carry with you or keep in your desk. Having it readily available ensures you can access these calming tools whenever you need a little pick-me-up.

Questions for Discussion:

1. Tell me about each item you chose.
2. Where do you want to keep your self-care companion kit?

Scan for video

3-6 Color Zone Emotion Drawing

Benefit: Identify feelings to gain mastery over emotions

Exercise Time: 30 minutes   **Ages:** Elementary 5+, middle school

Materials:
- Art journal
- Assorted drawing materials (markers, colored pencils, oil crayons)

Explanation:
Have you ever wondered how to express your feelings in a healthy way? The Emotion Zones are a helpful tool to understand different emotions. This framework uses colors to represent various emotional states, making it easier for everyone to recognize and communicate their feelings.

Steps:
1. Discuss each zone of emotion and the associated emotion.
2. Identify how to handle that particular emotion.
   - **Red Zone:** This zone is associated with **strong emotions**, like anger, frustration, and upset. It can feel like you're "seeing red" and might experience physical signs like racing heart or clenched fists. Remember, it's okay to feel these emotions, but it's important to express them in a healthy way that doesn't hurt yourself or others. Ways to move out of the red zone include taking a break, counting to 10, and talking about what happened.
   - **Yellow Zone:** The yellow zone represents **heightened emotions**, like excitement, silliness, or nervousness. You might feel like you have a lot of energy and might struggle to focus. It's helpful to find ways to manage your energy constructively in this zone. You can take a break, practice deep breathing, slow down, and consciously think before you act.
   - **Blue Zone:** This zone signifies **low energy emotions**, such as sadness, boredom, or tiredness. You might feel sluggish or unmotivated. Taking time to rest, relax, and engage in activities you enjoy can help you move out of the blue zone.
   - **Green Zone:** The green zone is the **ideal state for learning and focusing**. You feel calm, happy, and ready to engage with others. When you're in the green zone, you can effectively participate in classroom activities and build positive relationships.
3. Pick which color zone of emotion you are currently feeling.
4. Draw out a character practicing how to manage the current feeling.

Questions for Discussion:
1. Who are the people you can go to for help?
2. Have you been in the red or blue zone this week?

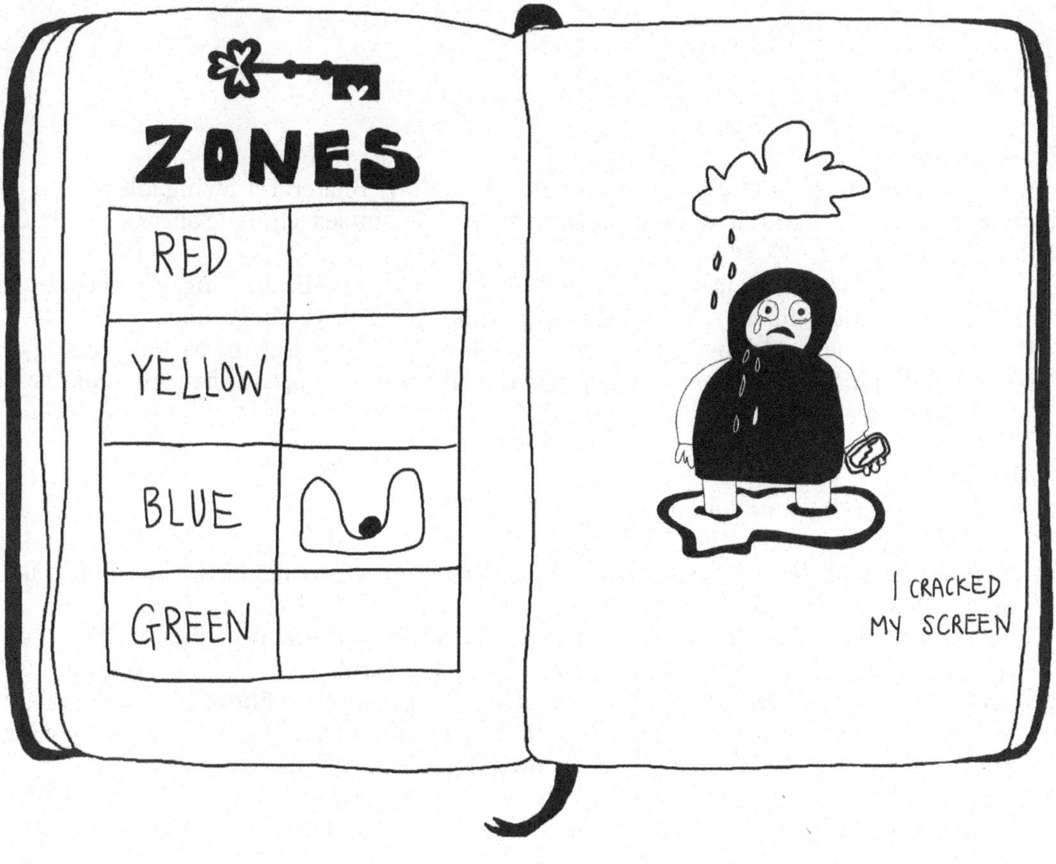
ZONES
RED
YELLOW
BLUE
GREEN
I CRACKED MY SCREEN

Scan for video

3-7 Butterfly Breath Drawing

Benefit: Regulates the nervous system and reduces stress

Exercise Time: 15 minutes

Ages: Elementary 5+, middle, and high school

Materials:
- Art journal
- Oil Crayon

Explanation:

Looking for an engaging way to get into the creative flow? Bilateral drawing allows you to loosen up using both hands to draw at the same time. This simple technique offers a multitude of benefits, including:

- Brain stimulation: By using both hands simultaneously while drawing, you activate and coordinate different brain regions, promoting cognitive integration.
- Nervous-system calming: The repetitive motions of bilateral drawing have a soothing effect, helping to reduce anxiety and promote relaxation by connecting hand movements to your breath.

Steps:

1. Choose two of the same colors.
2. Use both hands as you draw.
3. **Get comfortable:** Find a quiet and comfortable space. Sit up straight, with both feet flat on the floor.
4. **Connect with your breath:** Close your eyes, and take a few slow, deep breaths. Focus on the feeling of your chest rising and falling with each breath.
5. **Embrace the butterfly:** Imagine your hand transforming into a butterfly. Slowly trace a butterfly-like motion with both hands, starting from the center of the paper and moving upwards. As your hand moves up, **gently inhale** through your nose.
6. **Flow with the figure-eight:** As you reach the top of the paper, smoothly transition your hand movement into a continuous figure-eight pattern. While tracing the figure-eight, **exhale** slowly through your mouth.
7. **Repeat and connect:** Continue drawing the butterfly-figure-eight combination, synchronizing your breath with each movement. Focus on the feeling of calmness washing over you with each inhale and exhale.

Question for Discussion:

1. How did you feel when you started the drawing?
2. How do you feel now?

Scan for video

3-8 Emotion Sculptures

Benefit: Decreases stress and assists in identifying emotions

Exercise Time: 30 minutes

Ages: Elementary 5+, middle, and high school

Materials:
- Model magic (various colors)
- Refer to emotion list in the back of the book

Explanation:
Emotion sculptures are a unique way to translate your inner world into a tangible form. It's a visual language, allowing you to explore and express emotions through a combination of texture, color, and shape. Think of your sculptures as visual representations of specific feelings. You can use the emotion wheel as a guide, letting the different segments inspire your creation. Perhaps anger translates into sharp, jagged edges and fiery red hues, while joy might manifest as swirling, vibrant colors and playful curves.

Steps:
1. Create various colors by mixing model magic (red + blue = purple, blue + yellow = green, yellow + red = orange).
2. Match the color of the model magic to an emotion. The emotion chart is located in the back of the book.
3. Name the emotions you feel. Refer to page 196 to choose an emotion from the feeling list.
4. Create a sculpture that represents the feeling.
5. For each emotion, consider the size of it. If it's a big emotion, then it can be represented that way. Or if it's an emotion you don't feel often, it might be smaller.

Questions for Discussion:
1. Tell me about the colors and shapes.
2. Which feeling do you experience the most?

Scan for video

3-9 Emotional Landscape Painting

Benefit: Identifies feeling to help regulate emotions

Exercise Time: 30 minutes

Ages: Elementary 5+, middle, and high school

Materials:
- Art journal
- Pencil
- Watercolor
- Brushes
- Water holder

Explanation:

This exercise invites you to delve into the fascinating realm of emotional landscapes, where your inner world meets the external environment. Close your eyes for a moment, and tune into your current emotional state. What feeling is most prominent? Is it happiness, sadness, anger, or something else entirely? Now, imagine yourself stepping into a landscape that perfectly reflects your mood.

Steps:
1. Choose the weather, and draw out the background.
   - **Weather:** Is your emotional landscape bathed in the bright sunshine of joy, or is it stormy clouds of sadness? Perhaps it's swept by the windy gusts of anger or basking in the gentle breeze of contentment.
   - **Terrain:** Does your emotional landscape consist of towering mountains of worry or the winding path of uncertainty? Maybe it's a playful park full of laughter or a peaceful beach offering tranquility.
2. Next, choose the location, and draw out objects and landforms.
3. Then draw out details in the foreground.
4. Block in the drawing with watercolors.
5. Give it a title.

Questions for Discussion:
1. Does the landscape represent how you feel today?
2. How do you want to feel?
3. What steps can you take today to help you feel this way (e.g., go outside for a walk, read a book, or make art)?

Scan for video

3-10 Favorite Kind of Day Drawing

Benefit: Elevates mood and uses your imagination

Exercise Time: 30 minutes

Ages: Elementary 5+ , middle, and high school

Materials:
- Art journal
- Assorted drawing media (markers, colored pencils, oil crayons)

Explanation:
Have you ever closed your eyes and imagined yourself whisked away on an incredible adventure? What is your idea of a perfect day? Is it a day spent basking in the sun at the beach, surrounded by the sound of crashing waves? Perhaps it's a day hiking, riding your bike, visiting a city park, or maybe it's simply the joy of connecting with friends and making new memories.

Steps:
1. Take few moments, and conjure up fun memories or new experiences.
2. Draw out the experience.

Questions for Discussion:
1. When can you plan your next-favorite day experience?
2. Who do you want to share it with?

Scan for video

3-11 Release and Receive Painting

Benefit: Identifies goals

Exercise Time: 45 minutes

Ages: Elementary 8+, middle, and high school

Materials:
- Art journal
- Assorted drawing materials (markers, colored pencils, oil crayons)
- Acrylic paint
- Brushes

Explanation:

Ready to let go of negative emotions and embrace your best self. If you are holding on to feelings that aren't serving you, now is the time to release them. In this exercise, think of a situation that may feel uncomfortable to you. Name it, and release it as you draw it out on the hand. By releasing negativity and focusing on your aspirations, you open yourself up to attracting the thoughts, feelings, and experiences you truly want. On the other hand, you will identify what you want to bring; this allows you to open yourself up to thoughts, feelings, and actions you want to bring into your life.

Steps:

1. Trace both hands on each side of your journal.
2. On top of the left hand, write the word "**Release**" at the top of the page.
   - On the "Release" hand, what are the feelings that you want to release? Draw lines and shapes to release. You can write down the feelings and behaviors on each finger (e.g., fear, worry, sadness, jealousy, anger, saying mean things, yelling, etc.).
3. On top of the right hand, write the word "**Receive**"
   - On the "Receive" hand, what are the feelings that you want to bring in? Draw out lines and item you want to bring in.Write them on each finger (love, friendships, gratitude, joy, fun, peace, etc.).
4. Use paint to color in your hands.

Questions for Discussion:

1. Is there a particular word that stands out for you?
2. What have you learned about yourself in this exercise?
3. Take action on what you want to receive. What can you do to bring in the things you would like to experience?

Scan for video

3-12 Healing Container Drawing

Benefit: Identifying and processing emotions

Exercise Time: 30 minutes

Ages: Elementary 5+, middle, and high school

Materials:
- Art journal
- Assorted drawing materials (markers, colored pencils, oil crayons)
- Refer to Feeling list in the back of the book

Explanation:

Holding more than one emotion can feel overwhelming. In this art-journal technique, you can create a container to sort your emotions. You may feel sad *and* mad about a certain situation, such as a pet passing. Or maybe you got into trouble and were mad or sad that you were going to miss out on all the fun you had planned. When you take the time to create art about each emotion, it helps them not get bigger.

Steps:
1. Draw out a container in your journal (e.g., jar, bowl, vase).
2. Pick out 3 different emotions you may be feeling right now. Use the feeling chart on page 196 in the back of the book for reference.
3. Draw lines, colors, and shapes to represent those feelings in the container.
4. Color it in.

Questions for Discussion:
1. Which of the feelings is taking up the most space?
2. Do any feelings feel similar (e.g., excitement and anxiety)?

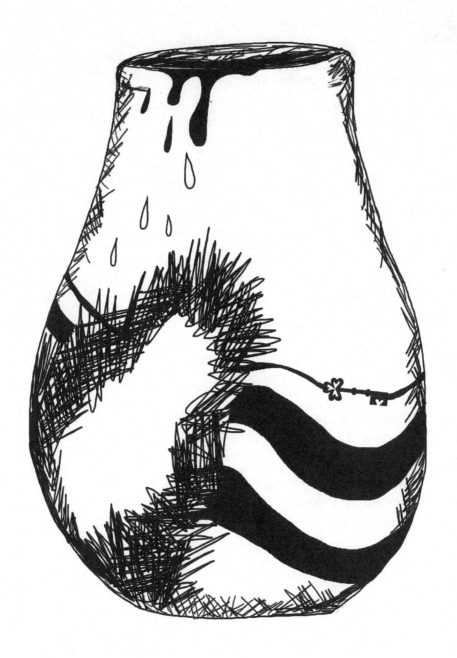

Scan for video

3-13 Calm and Cozy Corner

Benefit: Relieves stress and increases coping skills

Exercise Time: 30 minutes

Ages: Elementary 5+, middle, and high school

Materials:
- Bean bag chair
- Rug
- Stuffed animal
- Sensory toys
- Books
- Assorted art supplies
- Art journal

Explanation:

Transform a nook in your space into a personal refuge. This cozy corner can be your haven for relaxation and creativity. Here are some ideas to inspire you:
- Carve out a comfy spot to unwind. Think plush seating, like a bean bag or a comfy armchair.
- Surround yourself with things you love. Fill shelves with your favorite books, or display inspiring artwork.
- Spark your imagination. Consider a calming mural like rolling hills, or incorporate art supplies for creative expression.

Steps:
1. Set up cozy corner with items.
2. Use the cozy corner at a specific time of the day to wind down or when you need to relax.

Question for Discussion:
1. When would you like to use the cozy corner? What time of day?
2. Are there any other items do you think the cozy corner needs?

Scan for video

3-14 Body Drawing

Benefit: Builds self-awareness and understanding of self-concept

Exercise Time: 30 minutes

Ages: Elementary 5+, middle, and high school

Materials:
- Art journal
- Assorted drawing materials (markers, colored pencils, oil crayons)

Explanation:
Drawing the body is a fundamental skill for many artists. Here's why it's important:
- Expressing emotion: The human body is a powerful tool for storytelling. By understanding body language and posture, you can use figures in your art to convey emotions.
- Building a foundation: Mastering figure drawing is like a workout for your artistic skills. It hones observation, hand-eye coordination, and overall drawing technique. These skills benefit you in all areas of your artistic journey.

In short, drawing the body isn't just about creating realistic portraits. It's a way to convey emotion and create a visual narrative.

Steps:
1. Draw an oval for your head.
2. Draw a small square for your neck next to the oval.
3. Draw a large oval or square for the trunk of the body.
4. Draw two rectangles for the arms. Pose your figure to convey an emotion.
5. Draw two rectangles for the legs.
6. Draw the hands and feet as small squares.
7. Add facial features and hair.
8. Add clothes by drawing on top of the squares.
9. Reshape and erase lines as desired.
10. Add color and details to bring your figure to life.

Questions for Discussion
1. Who did you choose to draw?
2. Does the body language express emotion?

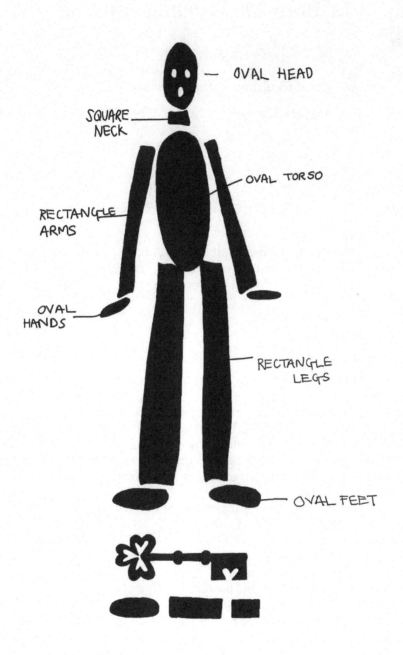

OVAL HEAD

SQUARE NECK

OVAL TORSO

RECTANGLE ARMS

OVAL HANDS

RECTANGLE LEGS

OVAL FEET

Scan for video

3-15 Body Map Feeling Painting

Benefit: Improves emotional regulation and coping skills

Exercise Time: 45 minutes (2 sessions)   **Ages:** Elementary 5+, middle, and high school

Materials:
- Art journal
- Large butcher paper
- Oil crayons
- Paint
- Brushes
- Painter's tape

Explanation:
Ever wonder how your emotions show up physically? A body map can help you visualize this connection! This exercise allows you to explore the many emotions you might be experiencing all at once. Use colors, shapes, and symbols to represent the different feelings you sense in various parts of your body.

Steps:
1. Create a list of all feelings (put timer on for 2 minutes). Refer to page 196 to choose a emotions from the feeling list.
2. Assign a color for each feeling on the list by placing a small dot of color next to the feeling word.
3. Pick 3 or 4 feelings to focus on, and ask the youth to discuss.
4. As you discuss each feeling, ask the individual to close their eyes (if they're comfortable with that), take a deep breath, and imagine where in their body the feeling is being felt.
5. Roll out butcher paper on the wall with tape. This can be modified if you don't have butcher paper and prefer to draw a body image in your art journal.
6. Use oil crayon to trace youth.
7. Use the color that represents the feeling; it may be in multiple areas of the body.
8. Block in color on the body with paint.

Questions for Discussion:
1. Can you tell me about your drawing?
2. What emotion is the one you feel the most?
3. Which emotion would you like to explore more?

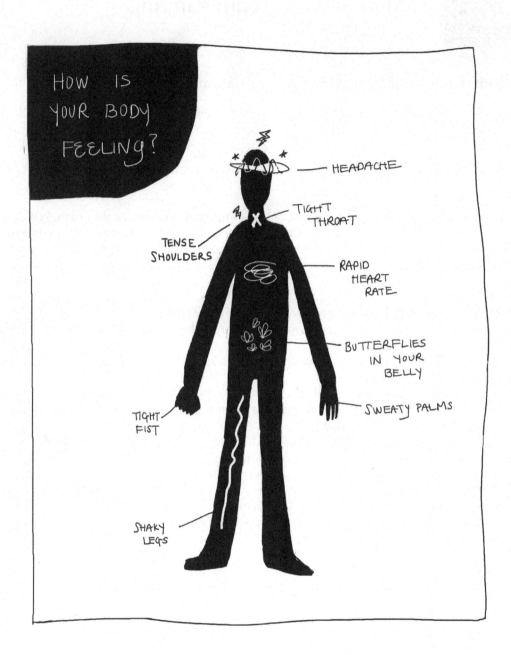

Scan for video

3-16 Rainbow Breath Painting

Benefit: Learn slow-breathing technique to decrease stress

Exercise Time: 15 minutes

Ages: Elementary 5+ and middle school

Materials:
- Art journal
- Watercolor set
- Brushes
- Water container

Explanation:
Close your eyes, and imagine your breath transforming into a magical paintbrush. With each inhale, draw one of the vibrant colors of the rainbow across the sky. As you exhale, come back across the same brush line with the same color. Repeat this exercise with each color of the rainbow. The colors of the rainbow are red, orange, yellow, green, blue, and purple.

Steps:
1. Dab your brush into the water and then into the color red.
2. Inhale through your nose as you move the red across the journal. Feel your tummy inflate like a red balloon.
3. Release your breath as you move your brush back across the art journal.
4. Clean your brush with water.
5. Dab your brush into the color orange.
6. Inhale through your nose as you move the orange across the journal. Feel your tummy inflate like an orange basketball.
7. Repeat for all the colors of the rainbow, ending with a peaceful, white cloud puff.
8. Draw out a surprise at the end of the rainbow.

Question for Discussion
1. Have you practiced breathing techniques before?
2. Where can you use this technique to help calm you down?

Scan for video

3-17 Constructive Destructive Chart Drawing

Benefit: Understand the difference between constructive and destructive behaviors

Exercise Time: 30 Minutes

Ages: Elementary 5+, middle, and high school

Materials:
- Art journal
- Assorted drawing materials (markers, colored pencils, gel pens)

Explanation:

We often focus on promoting good behaviors, but examining unhelpful ones can be equally as valuable. By analyzing both sides of the coin, we gain a deeper understanding of ourselves and of those around us. Here's why:

Understanding the "Why":

- Constructive Behaviors: Observe your positive reactions in situations that make you feel good. Examples include talking to someone, going for a walk, taking a time out, or making art.
- Destructive Behaviors: Observe negative actions that can lead to hurting you in some way. Examples include yelling when you don't get your way, avoiding talking about things that bother you, or name calling. It's important to look at behaviors to prevent repetition.

Steps:

1. Draw a line in your journal.
2. On the left-side top, write the word "Constructive."
3. On the right-side top, write the word "Destructive"
4. Draw, write, and discuss all the helpful behaviors on the constructive side of the chart.
5. Now, on the opposite side draw, write, and discuss all the destructive choices on the destructive side of the chart.

Questions for Discussion:

1. Which side has more words listed—the constructive or destructive side?
2. Can you add two more ideas to the "Helpful" side that you haven't tried?

CONSTRUCTIVE | DESTRUCTIVE

CONSTRUCTIVE

PAUSE

TAKE 3 DEEP BREATHS

ASK FOR HELP

TAKE A BREAK

ENJOY A WALK

CALM CORNER

`MAKE ART`

EXERCISE

_____

_____

DESTRUCTIVE

_____

_____

_____

YELLING

NAME CALLING

HITTING

BREAKING THINGS

Chapter 4

Taming Anger

*A*nger, *while a natural human emotion*, can sometimes feel like a raging inferno, threatening to consume everything in its path. But rather than letting it control you and be destructive, you will learn constructive, creative ways to help you tame your anger and cultivate inner peace.

Scan for video

4-1 Anger Thermometer Drawing

Benefit: Learn to rate your anger and gain control

Exercise Time: 30 minutes

Ages: Elementary 5+, middle, and high school

Materials:
- Art journal
- Markers

Explanation:
It's normal to feel angry when our needs aren't met. The anger thermometer can show you the different levels of anger. You will also explore what bothers you most. Try taking a moment to identify your anger level on a scale from one to one hundred. Ten represents mild annoyance, while one hundred signifies feeling ready to explode.

Steps:
1. Draw out your own anger thermometer (sample pictured here).
2. Review each anger feeling listed on the right of the side of the thermometer.
3. On the left side, give an example of something you've experienced to match the feeling.

Questions for Discussion:
1. Which one of these scenarios is happening most often?
2. What can you do to help you gain control of your anger?
3. What are ways to calm your anger before it gets bigger?

REASON

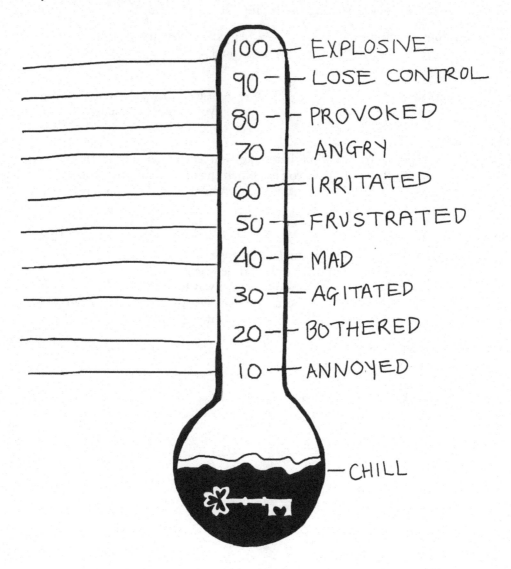

Scan for video

4-2 Set Off Drawing

Benefit: Promotes problem-solving and coping skills

Exercise Time: 45 minutes

Ages: Elementary 5+, middle, and high school

Materials:
- Art journal
- Assorted drawing media (markers, oil crayons, colored pencils)

Explanation:

A "set off" is a response to a situation that makes you feel bothered or upset. It may be when someone looks at you strange or calls you by something other than your name. If we lash out, it could lead to more trouble. Let's think and draw ways that can be constructive rather than destructive.

Steps:
1. Define what sets you off and how it relates to anger.
2. On the left hand side of the journal, draw a time when you were set off.
3. On the right side of the journal, draw out a better way to respond to the situation (get help from an adult, walk away from the situation, listen to understand, draw out how you feel, or ask for a moment to process information so that you can respond in a calm manner).

Questions for Discussion:
1. When was the last time you felt angry?
2. How do you cope with anger?
3. Who can you go to if you need help?

4-3 Anger Monster Drawing

Benefit: Improves emotional regulation and coping skills

Exercise Time: 45 minutes

Ages: Elementary 5+, middle, and high school

Materials:
- Art journal
- Assorted drawing media (markers, oil crayons, colored pencils)

Explanation:
This technique involves recognizing a hidden source of anger. Imagine all your past frustrations and hurts accumulating into a kind of "anger monster" within you. The size of this monster can vary from person to person. This concept allows you to visually see your anger as an extension of yourself.

Steps:
1. Think about your own anger. If your anger was a monster is it BIG or little?
2. Draw out your anger monster.
3. Add details to make it uniquely yours.

Questions for Discussion:
1. What is the name of your anger monster?
2. What message does the anger monster want to tell you?
3. What does your anger monster need to feel better?

Scan for video

4-4 Volcano Drawing

Benefit: Improves coping skills to manage anger

Exercise Time: 45 minutes

Ages: Elementary 5+, middle, and high school

Materials:
- Art journal
- Assorted drawing media (markers, oil crayons, colored pencils)

Explanation:
Think of anger like a volcano. Just as molten rock builds up pressure inside a volcano before erupting, frustration and irritation can simmer within us and result in angry outbursts. Creating an "anger volcano" is a creative outlet to explore these feelings in a safe and constructive way.

Steps:
1. Describe different ways people deal with anger. Are you a person that is explosive by acting out, yelling, or saying mean things to others? Or do you shut down, cry, withdraw, or stay quiet?
2. Start drawing your volcano by using a triangle shape.
3. Identify in the volcano drawing where your anger is located.
4. Represent your anger as the lava. Is it contained in the volcano or flowing out?

Questions for Discussion:
1. When have you felt angry or like a volcano?
2. Do you let the lava (feeling) build, or do you become explosive?

Scan for video

4-5 Exploding Volcano Sculpture

Benefit: Increase coping skills and your ability to regulate emotions

Exercise Time: 3 sessions of 45 minutes each **Ages:** Elementary 5+ and middle school

Materials:
- Newspaper
- Rigid wrap
- Bowl for water
- Tape
- Diet Coke (small bottle)
- Mentos
- Acrylic paint
- Brushes
- Palette
- Paper funnel

Explanation:

This activity makes dealing with anger fun and engaging. By creating a volcano sculpture, you get a sense of accomplishment. The most satisfying part is releasing your built-up tension in a safe and symbolic way. Are you holding in your anger like the lava in a volcano?

Steps:

1. Place newspaper down to protect the table.
2. Place Diet Coke bottle in center of newspaper.
3. Crumble newspaper to make balls that surround the Diet Coke bottle; make the base wider at the bottom and smaller as you go up.
4. Tape the paper balls around the Diet Coke.
5. Cut plaster wrap into strips.
6. Dip plaster wrap into the water, and put layers of the wrap on the newspaper.
7. Allow the plaster to dry for one day.
8. Paint the volcano.
9. Take the volcano outside for the explosion.
10. Open Diet Coke container.
11. Quickly put Mentos in a funnel and slide them into the Diet Coke.
12. Make sure to step back quickly to view the explosion.
13. Have someone take pictures of the experiment in action.

Question for Discussion:

1. Think about the volcano and how it exploded. What are some feelings that are beneath the surface that make you want to explode? Do you feel anger, hurt, disappointment, shame, scared, fearful, or anxious?
2. Have you been destructive with anger (e.g., called people names, hurt someone)?
3. What are ways you can de-escalate the anger?

Scan for video

4-6 Biggest Annoyance Drawing

Benefit: Increase coping skills

Exercise Time: 45 minutes

Ages: Elementary 5+, middle, and high school

Materials:
- Art journal
- Assorted drawing materials (markers, colored pencils, oil crayons)

Explanation:
Life throws us curveballs, big and small. Maybe it's a fight with a sibling, a tough assignment, or a frustrating video-game level. By acknowledging these annoyances early on, we can prevent them from snowballing into bigger problems. Taking a moment to explore these feelings can help us deal with them in a healthy way.

Steps:
1. Draw out your biggest annoyance.
2. If there is more than one, then draw the others as well.

Questions for Discussion:
1. How have you responded to the annoyance?
2. Who can you ask for help to resolve the problem (parent, teacher, friend)?
3. If you can't change the situation, can you find ways within yourself to deal better with the issue?

Scan for video

4-7 Destruct and Construct
Mixed Media Collage

Benefit: Identifies feelings and increases problem-solving skills

Exercise Time: 45 minutes

Ages: Elementary 5+, middle, and high school

Materials:
- Art journal
- Assorted drawing media (markers, oil crayons, colored pencils)
- Acrylic paint
- Brushes
- Water container
- Glue stick

Explanation:

This exercise can help you let go of frustration that is weighing you down and create a more positive outlook. Acknowledge the feeling you want to release by drawing it out and then ripping it up! Now, you can rebuild, using the pieces to construct a new feeling, representing a fresh perspective.

Steps:
1. Draw out current emotions with drawing media in the journal.
2. Rip up the drawing.
3. Create a new image with the ripped pieces.
4. Glue the pieces in your journal.
5. Add paint to bring out the new image.

Questions for Discussion:
1. How did you feel when you started?
2. How are you feeling now?

Scan for video

4-8 Anger Selfie Mixed Media Collage

Benefit: Improves self-awareness, emotion regulation, and coping skills

Exercise Time: 45 minutes

Ages: Elementary 5+, middle, and high school

Materials:
- Art journal
- Printed picture of self with angry expression
- Assorted drawing media (markers, oil crayons, colored pencils)
- Acrylic paint
- Brushes
- Water container
- Glue stick
- Scissors

Explanation:

Feeling furious? Anger is a powerful emotion, and it's totally normal to experience it. Close your eyes, and think about a recent time when you felt really mad. What did it feel like in your body? Did your hands clench? Did your breath speed up? Did your face scrunch up?

Steps:
1. Take a picture of yourself with an angry face.
2. Print image (black-and-white works).
3. Cut out your face from the page.
4. Glue to journal.
5. Use bold colors, sharp lines, or anything that expresses your anger in a creative way to paint around the cutout of your face.

Questions for Discussion:
1. When was the last time you felt anger take over?
2. What happened?
3. What's another way to deal with it constructively?

Scan for video

4-9 Anger Feeling Feltie Plushie

Benefit: Increases self-awareness and coping skills

Exercise Time: 2 sessions of 45 minutes each

Ages: Elementary 5+, and middle school

Materials:
- Felt
- Hot glue (or needles and thread)
- Pins
- Paper for template
- Polyester filling
- Scissors
- Anger-monster drawing for inspiration
- Paper

Explanation:
When you feel frustrated or upset, it's normal to get angry. An anger-monster plushie can be a fun tool to help you understand and deal with your anger in a healthy way. Here's how it can work: Imagine all your annoyance and frustration going into the plushie. This way, you're not bottling it up inside, and you have a cuddly reminder to take a breath and calm down. Plus, having a silly plushie to focus on might make it easier to see things from a different perspective.

Steps:
1. Use your anger-monster drawing as inspiration for the shape and form of your plushie, or draw a new form for your anger plushie.
2. Trace out the shape onto paper to use as a template.
3. Place felt under your drawing as a template.
4. Use pins to hold in place, and cut the felt.
5. Repeat the last step, to create a front side and a back side of the plushie.
6. You can hot-glue edges on the inside or sew together pieces.
7. Leave a space open to fill the stuffing.
8. If you are using glue, make sure it is dry completely before moving to the next step.
9. Add details with felt by attaching eyes, ears, clothing, horns, tail, etc.

Questions for Discussion:
1. What is your anger plushie's name?
2. What makes it come alive?
3. Is there something the Anger Feeling Feltie would like to say to you or someone else?
4. What does it need to feel better?

Scan for video

4-10 Self-Compassion Feeling Feltie Plushie

Benefit: Increases self-awareness and coping skills

Exercise Time: 2 sessions of 45 minutes each

Ages: Elementary 5+ and middle school

Materials:
- Felt
- Hot glue (or needles and thread)
- Pins
- Paper for template
- Polyester filling
- Scissors
- Paper

Explanation:

Self-compassion is about being nice to yourself even when you mess up. We can easily be mean and mad at ourselves if things don't go our way. We may even call ourselves names. My self-compassion plushie is called "Hug." Your self-compassion plushie is here to give you support and remind you to be kinder to yourself.

Steps:
1. Draw out the shape you would want your self-compassion plushie to be.
2. Trace out the shape onto paper to use as a template.
3. Place felt under the paper template, pin the felt to the paper, and cut out.
4. Repeat the last step, so that you have both a front side and a back side of the plushie.
5. You can hot-glue edges on the inside or sew together pieces.
6. Leave space to fill with stuffing.
7. Add details with felt, and attach eyes, ears, clothing, horns, tail, etc.

Questions for Discussion:
1. What is your self-compassion plushie's name?
2. When do you give yourself a hard time?
3. What can you do to be kinder to yourself?

Chapter 5

Keys to Releasing Stress, Worry, and Anxiety

W*orry and anxiety can linger in our minds,* casting a shadow over our days. We can learn to release these pesky emotions and reclaim inner peace by using art to express our feelings. Here are creative techniques to help you unburden your mind.

Scan for video

5-1 Repetition Is Key Drawing

Benefit: Reduces anxiety and increases mindfulness

Exercise Time: 20–45 minutes

Ages: Elementary 5+, middle, and high school

Materials:
- ● Art journal
- ● Assorted drawing materials (markers, oil crayons, colored pencils)

Explanation:
Are you feeling anxious? Anxiety is when you worry about something that hasn't happened yet and you're unsure of the outcome. Doodling calming patterns can help quiet the mind. Repetitive patterns can be a great way to focus attention and ease anxiety. Take a break, and get lost in the rhythm of drawing repetitive patterns.

Steps:
1. Check in with yourself; rate your anxiety on a scale of one to ten, with ten being very anxious and one being calm. What number are you today?
2. Follow the guided pattern, or create a unique pattern.
3. Fill the page with the pattern.
4. Add color if you wish.

Question for Discussion:
1. Let's check in. What is your anxiety level now?
2. Did you enjoy doodling?

Scan for video

5-2 Healing Mandala Painting

Benefit: Increases mindfulness and decreases stress

Exercise Time: 45 minutes

Ages: Elementary 5+, middle, and high school

Materials:
- Art journal
- Assorted drawing media (markers, oil crayons, colored pencils)
- Watercolor set
- Water container
- Ruler

Explanation:
We often worry about the future, which can feel out of control. Mandalas, with their beautiful, centered designs, have been used for centuries to help people focus on the present moment. By quieting the mind and bringing our attention inward, mandalas can naturally calm our nervous system and ease anxiety.

Steps:
1. Check in with yourself; rate your anxiety on a scale of one to ten, with ten being very anxious and one being calm. What number are you today?
2. Draw a large circle in the journal (trace a small bowl if needed).
3. Split the circle into four sections with a ruler.
4. Create repeating shapes in each section.
5. Fill in with watercolor.

Questions for Discussion:
1. Let's check in. What is your anxiety level now?
2. What do the symbols you chose mean to you?
3. Can you tell me more about the colors you chose?

Scan for video

5-3 Worry Monster Drawing

Benefit: Develops emotional regulation and coping skills

Exercise Time: 2 sessions of 45 minutes each

Ages: Elementary 5+, middle, and high school

Materials:
- Art journal
- Assorted drawing materials (markers, oil crayons, colored pencils)

Explanation:

It's normal to worry sometimes. Worries can feel a bit overwhelming, but it shouldn't take over all your thoughts. If you're feeling overwhelmed by emotions, try creating your own worry monster. It's a fun way to face those worries head-on. Giving your worries a physical form can help you manage the emotion.

Steps:

1. What does your worry monster look like? Is it BIG or little?
2. Draw the worry monster in the journal.
3. Add details to make it uniquely yours.

Questions for Discussion:

1. What do you worry about?
2. Is this something you think about daily?
3. What steps can you take to lessen that worry?

Scan for video

5-4 Wash the Worry Painting

Benefit: Increases coping skills

Exercise Time: 30 minutes

Ages: Elementary 8+, middle, and high school

Materials:
- Art journal
- Assorted drawing media (markers, oil crayons, colored pencils)
- Acrylic Paint
- Brushes
- Water Container

Explanation:
This exercise is a place to confront things that are troubling you. Let's get rid of this burden by describing and writing your worries in a circle. The circle is a symbolic container to hold your thoughts and feelings. Then, you will paint on the circle and put the worry behind you.

Steps:
1. Draw a circle.
2. Write the things that cause worry in the circle.
3. Choose a paint color to symbolize worry.
4. Cover up the words using broad and expressive brushstrokes.
5. Wash away your worry with color and design.

Questions for Discussion:
1. Do you want to share what was in your circle?
2. Are you comforted by the fact that you can use this technique anytime you want to let go of thoughts that are bothering you?

Scan for video

5-5 Let It Flow Mixed Media

Benefit: Reduces anxiety

Exercise Time: 30 minutes

Ages: Elementary 5+, middle, and high school

Materials:
- Canvas board
- Art journal
- Pencil
- Box of crayons
- Hot glue
- Hot-glue sticks
- Blow-dryer or hot-air gun
- Butcher paper to protect the floor

Explanation:

Feeling stressed? Sometimes we worry about things we can't control, which can make us feel stuck. The good news is, we have control over how we see things. This art exercise isn't about changing reality but about changing your perspective. Think of something outside your control, something that makes you feel tense. Now, imagine how you'd like things to feel instead—calm, flowing, maybe even joyful. This exercise represents allowing yourself to flow and release control.

Steps:
1. Write out what you would like to change or control in your journal.
2. Brainstorm other ways to view the situation, and write those down, too.
3. Attach crayons individually on top of the canvas with hot glue.
4. Prop canvas against the wall.
5. Place the butcher paper on the floor to catch wet crayon droppings.
6. Use the blow-dryer on crayons, and watch the flow of color drip down the canvas.

Questions for Discussion:
1. What are areas of your life you can't control?
2. What ideas do you have for changing your perspective on these areas of life you can't control?

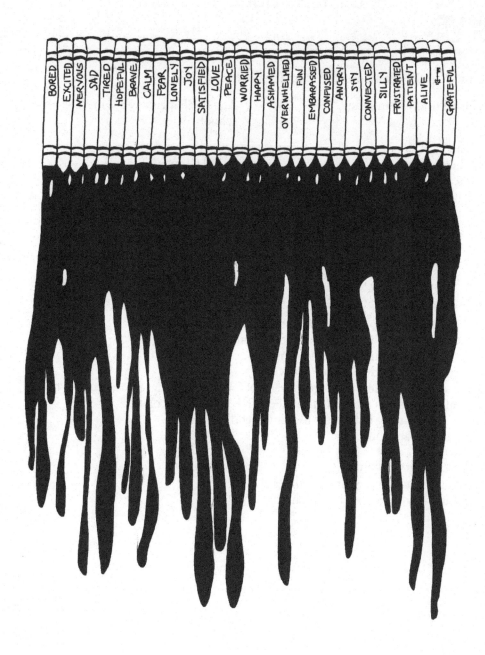

Scan for video

5-6 Bilateral Butterfly Painting

Benefit: Regulate emotions and calm the nervous system

Exercise Time: 30 minutes

Ages: Elementary 5+, middle, and high school

Materials:
- Butcher paper
- Painter's tape
- Acrylic
- Oil Crayons
- Water container
- Brushes

Explanation:
Remember in exercise 3–7, Butterfly Breath, how we connected our breath to drawing strokes in your journal? Now, let's take it up a notch. This time, we'll use our whole body to move with our breath, creating a bigger, more-expressive connection.

Steps:
1. Use painter's tape to hang up large butcher paper on the wall.
2. Use oil crayon in both hands to start the bilateral drawing.
3. Breathe in; make large movements with both arms to start the two wings of the butterfly. Use your whole body to create the wings.
4. Breathe out; make another large movement for the two wings for the bottom of the butterfly.
5. Repeat this process multiple times. Feel free to use new colors.
6. Make shapes using both arms to create details.
7. Paint in the large butterfly.

Questions for Discussion:
1. Did you enjoy making a large painting?
2. Do you know what butterflies symbolize?

Scan for video

5-7 Nature Heals Painting

Benefit: Improves mindfulness and relaxation, and reduces stress.

Exercise Time: 45 minutes   **Ages:** Elementary, middle, and high school

Materials:
- Organic object found in nature
- Art journal
- Assorted drawing media (pencil, oil crayon, colored pencil)
- Watercolor
- Water container
- Brushes

Explanation:
Nature is bursting with inspiration waiting to be discovered. Embark on an adventure, and find an object that sparks your curiosity. It could be a smooth stone, a vibrant flower, a beautiful feather, or a curiously shaped leaf. Bring your newfound treasure back, and use it as your inspiration for a drawing.

Steps:
1. Go outside and find an object to use for inspiration to draw.
2. Observe the details in the object.
3. Draw it out to the best of your ability. This isn't about making a perfect picture.
4. Repeat drawing the object to create a pattern.
5. Add the details and your own creative expression. Add other items or objects from the environment to make your image unique.
6. Paint in your object with watercolor paint.

Questions for Discussion:
1. What are other objects that inspire you in nature?
2. Name feelings associated with nature.

Scan for video

5-8 Worry Window Drawing

Benefit: Reduce worry and increase coping skills

Exercise Time: 15 minutes

Ages: Elementary 5+, middle, and high school

Materials:
- Art journal
- Assorted drawing media (markers, oil crayons, colored pencils)

Explanation:
Have your worries run wild? Here's a trick. Instead of letting them run wild all day, give them a designated time slot. Set a timer for 15 minutes, and use that time to really dig into what is worrying you. Write down your worries, draw them out—whatever helps you understand them better. Once the timer goes off, it's worry-free time. Shift your focus back to the present moment, and leave those worries in their designated window. You can always revisit them tomorrow, if needed, but, for now, enjoy the peace of mind.

Steps:
1. Draw out a window.
2. In each windowpane, draw out a worry.
3. Color it in.
4. Discuss the worry.

Questions for Discussion:
1. Which worry takes up the most space in your head?
2. What can we do today to shift our focus away from the worry (go outside, make some art, read a book, etc.)?

Scan for video

5-9 Anxiety Selfie Mixed Media Collage

Benefit: Improves self-awareness, emotion regulation, and coping skills

Exercise Time: 45 minutes

Ages: Elementary 5+, middle, and high school

Materials:
- Art journal
- Assorted drawing materials (markers, oil crayons, colored pencils)
- Collage material (magazines, colored paper)
- Printed picture of self with an anxious face
- Scissors
- Glue

Explanation:

Feeling tangled in thoughts? Collage-making can be the key to untangling anxious thoughts. Cut, tear, and glue images that capture your anxiety, letting the chaos spill onto the page. By giving your worries a physical form, you can begin to release them. It's a visual release, a way to see the anxiety, own it, and let it go.

Steps:
1. Take a picture of yourself with an anxious face.
2. Print selfie picture.
3. Cut out your face from the background.
4. Glue your face image to the journal.
5. Look for collage images of pictures or words related to anxiety.
6. Glue the images to the journal.
7. Use assorted drawing media to color it in.

Questions for Discussion:
1. What makes you anxious?
2. What stands out most in the image?

Scan for video

5-10 Worried Feeling Feltie Plushie

Benefit: Increases awareness of feelings and coping skills

Exercise Time: 45 minutes   **Ages:** Elementary 5+, and middle school

Materials:
- Felt
- Hot glue (or needles and thread)
- Polyester filling
- Scissors
- Worry-monster drawing
- Paper

Explanation:
Everyone needs a hug from time to time. Plushies can be more than just toys. They can be a source of comfort and security, a little friend to hold close when you're feeling down. Let's make a small plushie to fit right in your pocket—a huggable friend that can travel with you wherever you go.

Steps:
1. Use the worry-monster drawing as inspiration for the shape and form of the worry plushie, or draw a new shape.
2. Trace out the shape onto paper to use as a template.
3. Place felt under template, and use pins to hold it in place.
4. Cut the felt.
5. Repeat the last step for the front side and back side of the plushie.
6. Hot-glue edges on the inside or sew together pieces.
7. Leave space to add stuffing.
8. Add details with felt, and attach (eyes, ears, clothing, hat, etc.).

Questions for Discussion:
1. What are your favorite comforting items?
2. Where would you like to keep the plushie?

Chapter 6

Holding Sadness and Grief

Holding sadness and grief is not about pretending or ignoring your emotions. It's okay to acknowledge pain, embrace vulnerability, and grieve. This is an opportunity to feel your emotion and express it creatively.

Scan for video

6-1 Grief Bowl Sculpture

Benefit: Learning to process grief

Exercise Time: 60 minutes

Ages: Elementary 5+, middle, and high school

Materials:
- Plastic bowl
- Plaster wrap
- Plastic wrap
- Acrylic paint
- Brushes
- Paper plates
- Butcher paper

Explanation:

Grief can be a big, messy feeling, especially after losing someone we love. A Grief Bowl can be a special way to help us manage those emotions. It's a safe space to put our sadness, anger, or any other feelings we might be having. Design the Grief Bowl in a way that feels special to you. Add details that symbolize your loved one and happy memories. It's a personal way to remember them and keep them close.

Steps:
1. Turn plastic bowl upside down (use it as the shape for the bowl).
2. Wrap plastic bowl with cellophane.
3. Cut plaster wrap into strips.
4. Layer plaster wrap onto cellophane-wrapped bowl.
5. Allow 10–15 minutes to dry.
6. Take off the new plaster bowl from the plastic mold.
7. Make a mark on the bowl that represents your sadness on the bowl.
8. Paint the bowl with loved one's favorite color, or paint objects that they loved on the bowl.

Question for Discussion:
1. The bowl can be used to place special items from your loved one. Do you have a special item to place in the bowl?
2. What is a favorite memory with your loved one?

Scan for video

6-2 Favorite Memory Drawing

Benefit: Increases positive emotions and helps process memories

Exercise Time: 30 minutes

Ages: Elementary 5+, middle, and high school

Materials:
- Art journal
- Assorted drawing material (markers, oil crayons, colored pencils)

Explanation:
Let's celebrate love! Take a moment to remember a special person in your life. Was there a favorite activity you shared, a funny inside joke, or just a time you enjoyed being together? Close your eyes, and picture that happy memory. Now, grab your art supplies, and bring that memory to life with a drawing. It could be a specific scene or just a feeling you want to capture.

Steps:
1. Reflect on a cherished memory of your loved one.
2. Is there a favorite color associated with this person or something that they loved to do (e.g., cooking, gardening, watching TV, etc.)?
3. Draw out the memory in the art journal.

Question for Discussion:
1. Plan to do something now to honor a loved one. For example, if the loved one enjoyed baking, you can spend some time baking, too.
2. What are other ways to honor your loved one?

Scan for video

6-3 Sad and Mad Collage

Benefit: Identifies feelings and improves decision making

Exercise Time: 45 minutes   **Ages:** Elementary 5+ and middle school

Materials:
- *Rad is SMAD!!* book
- Collage materials (assorted paper, magazines)
- Scissors
- Glue stick
- Art journal
- Assorted drawing material (markers, oil crayons, colored pencils)

Explanation:

Life throws a lot of feelings our way, and sometimes they can all come at once. The monster truck, Rad, was sad that he did't have any friends to cruise with, and he acted out angrily. Art can be a great way to explore mixed emotions. Use your creativity to express both the sadness and the feeling of anger in a constructive way.

Steps:
1. Watch *Rad is SMAD!!* book in video.
2. Pick a color for mad.
3. Pick a color for sad.
4. Using the colors you chose for mad and sad, cut up magazines or colored paper using those colors.
5. Create an image with pieces of both colors in the art journal.

Questions for Discussion:
1. Which color is most dominant in the art?
2. Which feeling is most present—sad or mad?
3. What was constructed with the new pieces?

Scan for video

6-4 Origami Memory Box Mixed Media

Benefit: Supports processing grief and improves coping skills

Exercise Time: 45 minutes

Ages: Elementary 5+, middle, and high school

Materials:
- 9"x12" paper
- Scissors
- Glue
- Picture of loved one
- Assorted drawing media (markers, oil crayons, colored pencils)

Explanation:

Folding an origami memory box can be a calming way to remember someone special. The process of creating the box is fun. You can fill the box with cherished mementos or photos as a memory box.

Steps:
1. Fold and cut paper to make it into a square.
2. Watch video for step-by-step process to make lid.
3. Repeat the folding process to make bottom of box.
4. Add your favorite photos.
5. Design the box.

Questions for Discussion:
1. Tell me more about your memories with the loved one.
2. What will be placed in the box?
3. Do you want to give it to someone special?

Scan for video

6-5 Felt Heart Messages Mixed Media

Benefit: Increases positive emotions and connections

Exercise Time: 45 minutes

Ages: Elementary 5+, middle, and high school

Materials:
- 8"x8" felt
- Scissors
- Markers
- Polyester stuffing
- Hot glue (or needle and thread)
- Paper for making heart-shape outline

Explanation:

Felt hearts are a fun way to express love and connection any time of the year. You can stitch a word onto the heart, like "brave" or "grateful," as a reminder of your strengths, and spread positive messages to others.

Steps:
1. Draw out a heart shape on paper as the template.
2. Cut out the heart shape template.
3. Draw out heart shape on felt.
4. Cut out two hearts from felt to create a front and back.
5. Stitch a strength word onto one of the hearts.
6. Sew two hearts together, or use hot glue to attach.
7. Leave a space for stuffing.
8. Fill the heart with polyester stuffing.
9. Stitch or hot-glue heart.

Questions for Discussion:
1. How many hearts would you like to make?
2. Is there someone you know who could use a heart to feel better?

Scan for video

6-6 Inside and Outside Mask Sculpture

Benefit: Improves self-awareness, emotion regulation, and coping skills

Exercise Time: 3 sessions of 45 minutes each

Ages: Elementary 5+, middle, and high school

Materials:
- Tin-foil sheets
- Scissors
- Rigid wrap
- Bowl
- Water
- String
- Acrylic paint
- Pencil
- Art journal

Explanation:

Grief and sadness come in waves, sometimes unpredictably. One moment, you might feel great, and the next, a memory washes over you that brings sadness. In this exercise, a mask is used as a metaphor to address the emotions that you are experiencing. On the inside, you can paint the emotions you're feeling inside (sadness, maybe anger, or a mix). On the outside, you can design what you want to show the world—or, maybe, how you'd like to feel eventually.

Steps:

1. Draw out mask shape.
2. Use large piece of foil.
3. Press the tin foil against the youth's face to trace face shape and eye holes.
4. Place tin foil on table.
5. Cut out eye holes with scissors and shape of mask.
6. Next, cut strips of the rigid wrap.
7. Dip the rigid wrap into the water to activate the plaster.
8. Rub the rigid wrap to get rid of gauze holes.
9. Place the rigid wrap on top of the foil with three layers for thickness.
10. Cover both sides, and let dry for a day.
11. Discuss current feelings, and use colors to match those feeling with paint on the inside of the mask.
12. On the outside of the mask, design and decorate the feeling expressed to others.
13. Attach string on the side to hang or wear.

Questions for Discussion:

1. What do the colors you chose mean to you?
2. Try on your mask. Where would you like to wear your mask?

Scan for video

6-7 Feel-Better Pillow

Benefit: Reduces stress and increases coping skills

Exercise Time: 45 minutes

Ages: Elementary 5+, middle, and high school

Materials:
- Felt squares
- Scissors
- Polyester stuffing
- Hot glue (or needle and thread)
- Markers

Explanation:

Making a feel-good pillow is a way to reduce stress. It is a creative way to calm down. These pillows are perfect for snuggling with when you need a little pick-me-up or to calm down. You can personalize your pillow by adding your initials or name on the front, making them extra special.

Steps:
1. Pick out favorite colors for the pillow.
2. Choose colors for the letters of the pillow.
3. Draw out letters with markers on felt.
4. Cut felt letters.
5. Sew or use hot-glue gun to attach letter(s).
6. Place two felt pieces together for pillow.
7. Sew or use hot-glue gun to attach both pieces, leaving space for stuffing.
8. Stuff pillow with polyester.
9. Stitch or hot-glue stuffing hole.

Questions for Discussion:
1. When is a good time to use the pillow?
2. Where would the pillow be kept?

Scan for video

6-8 Sadness Monster Drawing

Benefit: Improves self-awareness, emotion regulation, and coping skills

Exercise Time: 45 minutes

Ages: Elementary 5+, middle, and high school

Materials:
- Art journal
- Assorted art media (markers, oil pastels, colored pencils)

Explanation:
We all feel sad sometimes. Maybe you've lost something special, are feeling lonely, or made a mistake. Those things can definitely bring on sadness, but it doesn't mean there's anything wrong with you. The key is to acknowledge those sad feelings instead of bottling them up. This exercise is a great way to explore sadness and let it out in a healthy way.

Steps:
1. Pick a color that represents sadness.
2. Draw out a monster to represent sadness or disappointment.
3. Use assorted drawing materials to add details to the sadness monster.
4. Add words to the drawing.

Questions for Discussion:
1. What's the name of the sadness monster?
2. Tell me more about the color and details you added.
3. When was the last time you felt sad?

Scan for video

6-9 Sadness Selfie Mixed Media Collage

Benefit: Improves self-awareness, emotion regulation, and coping skills

Exercise Time: 45 minutes

Ages: Elementary 5+, middle, and high school

Materials:
- Art journal
- Take picture of disappointed face
- Print picture (black-and-white image works)
- Glue stick
- Scissors
- Acrylic paint
- Oil crayons

Explanation:

Things don't always work out the way we want them to. Maybe you didn't get something you wanted, or plans fell through. It's totally normal to feel disappointed. If we don't acknowledge those feelings, they can build up. This exercise is a chance to explore disappointment in a creative way. Think about what made you feel disappointed, and then use colors and lines to express that feeling on paper. It's okay to get a little messy.

Steps:
1. Take a photo of a disappointed or sad face.
2. Print the image.
3. Cut away the background and glue into the art journal.
4. Add lines, shapes, and colors to express your disappointment.
5. Add text to the image.

Questions for Discussion:
1. When was the last time you were disappointed?
2. What activities can you do to make yourself feel better?

Scan for video

6-10 Sadness Feeling Feltie Plushie

Benefit: Increases awareness of feelings and develops coping skills

Exercise Time: 2 sessions of 45 minutes each

Ages: Elementary 5+, middle, and high school

Materials:
- Felt
- Hot glue (or needles and thread)
- Polyester filling
- Scissors
- Sadness-monster drawing for inspiration
- Paper

Explanation:

Ever feel a little blue? Making a sadness plushie is a way to express those feelings and give them a cuddly form. Sometimes it's easier to deal with something when you can see it, rather than just feeling it on the inside. Your plushie can be a reminder that it's okay to feel sad. It can be a good way to confront those emotions and a friend to snuggle with when you need a pick-me-up.

Steps:
1. Use sadness-monster drawing as inspiration for the shape, color, and form of the plushie.
2. Trace out the shape onto paper to use as a template.
3. Place felt under template and pin it to keep it in place.
4. Cut felt.
5. Repeat the last step, to create a front side and a back side of the sadness plushie.
6. Hot-glue edges on the inside or sew together pieces.
7. Leave space to fill stuffing.
8. Add details with felt and attach (eyes, ears, clothing, horns, tail, etc.)

Questions for Discussion:
1. What is the plushie's name?
2. If the plushie had a message, what would it be?
3. Where will you keep the plushie?

Chapter 7

Effective Decision Making

Decision making is an important skill. In this chapter, we will identify a challenge or an obstacle, gather information, and figure out alternative ways to solve problems, empowering you to make the best choices possible. Having good decision-making skills will provide you with the best outcome when faced with tough situations.

Scan for video

7-1 Before-During-After Drawing

Benefit: Increases problem-solving skills and self-reflection

Exercise Time: 45 minutes

Ages: Elementary 5+, middle, and high school

Materials:
- Art journal
- Assorted drawing media (markers, oil crayons, colored pencils)

Explanation:
When something happens that leaves us wishing we'd acted differently—perhaps a disagreement with a friend, a moment of frustration, or a mistake we made. Instead of carrying that frustration with you, it's important to take a step back and reflect on what happened. Think about what led up to the situation and how you might handle it differently next time. By understanding the root cause and exploring alternative responses, we can learn and grow from our experiences.

Steps:
1. Make three rectangles in your art journal.
2. Label the boxes "Before," During," and "After."
3. In the first box, draw out what caused the problem.
4. In the second box, draw out your response to the problem.
5. In the third box, draw out a new solution or a better way to respond.

Questions for Discussion:
1. How do you feel now about the incident?
2. What are other alternative ways you could respond?
3. Who can you get help from next time?

Scan for video

7-2 Life Wheel Drawing

Benefit: Improves self-awareness and organizational skills

Exercise Time: 45 minutes

Ages: Elementary 8+, middle, and high school

Materials:
- Art journal
- Assorted drawing media (markers, oil crayons, colored pencils)

Explanation:
In this exercise, we explore what your typical day looks like. There are days when we have many obligations to complete and days when we have lots of free time. Right now, we want to focus on a normal day. This will give you some perspective on what you spend your free time on and how to make the best use of that time.

Steps:
1. Make a list of daily activities: sleeping, school, homework, extracurricular activities, online, hobbies, obligations, time with family and friends.
2. Draw a circle in the journal.
3. Divide the circle into slices.
4. In the slices, write and draw out things you do in your day.
5. Each slice will be a different size, according to the time spent doing them.

Questions for Discussion:
1. Are you surprised to learn something new about yourself?
2. How are you spending your free time?
3. Are you making time to be outside?
4. Have you thought of new hobbies that you would like to incorporate into your week?

Scan for video

7-3 Clay Coil Pot Sculpture

Benefit: Improves problem-solving skills

Exercise Time: 3 sessions of 45 minutes each (plus drying time)

Ages: Elementary, middle, and high school

Materials:

- Self-drying clay
- Clay tools (rolling pin, wood shaper)
- Acrylics
- Paint
- Soil
- Plant
- Brushes

Explanation:

This exercise highlights the power of a growth mindset. A growth mindset is the belief that you can improve with effort, learning, and persistence. It's about having a positive attitude and embracing challenges, just like a house plant needs the right environment to flourish—water, sunlight, good soil, and a pot to grow in. But what if things don't always go our way? That's where a growth mindset comes in. When faced with challenges, we can use our problem-solving skills to find creative solutions.

Steps:

1. Cut slab of clay.
2. Roll out a base for your pot.
3. Cut out a circle for the base.
4. Cut smaller pieces of clay to use for coils.
5. Roll clay to make coils.
6. Press a coil of clay around circular base.
7. Add coils on top of each other to build the pot.
8. Allow clay to dry.
9. Paint pot.
10. Place soil in pot.
11. Plant a clipping in the soil.
12. Watch it grow.

Questions for Discussion:

1. Give an example of when you practiced growth mindset.
2. If you need help, can you tell me two other ways to get support?

Scan for video

7-4 Growth Mindset Plant Painting

Benefit: Improves problem-solving skills

Exercise Time: 45 minutes

Ages: Elementary 5+, middle, and high school

Materials:
- Pencil
- Art journal
- Plant (or picture of a plant from internet)
- Acrylic paint
- Brushes
- Water container

Explanation:
When things don't go as planned, we feel frustrated or disappointed. This can lead to feeling stuck or discouraged. Imagine yourself as a plant. Plants need light and water to grow big and strong, just like we need a positive attitude to overcome challenges. When we have a fixed mindset, it's like being in a dark room where we can't see a solution—plants need sunlight to grow. We need to shed light on the situation and face our challenges.

Here's the good news: we can all develop a growth mindset. Instead of getting upset about a setback, we can try to see it as an opportunity to learn and find solutions. By focusing on solutions and staying positive, we can develop the resilience to overcome any obstacle.

Steps:
1. Use an actual plant, or look up a plant on the internet (favorite flower, succulent, or house plant).
2. Sketch out plant with pencil onto the canvas.
3. Discuss situations that represent a fixed mindset.
4. Discuss ways to use a growth mindset.
5. Paint the plant by blocking in colors.

Questions for Discussion:
1. Give an example of a fixed-mindset situation.
2. Give an example of a growth-mindset situation.

Scan for video

7-5 Love and Hate Collage

Benefit: Improves self-awareness, emotion regulation, and coping skills

Exercise Time: 45 minutes

Ages: Elementary 5+, middle, and high school

Materials:
- Magazines or print image from internet
- Scissors
- Glue
- Art journal
- Assorted drawing materials

Explanation:

Life is full of experiences, both wonderful and challenging. Some things bring us joy, while others might make us feel uncomfortable or frustrated. This art exercise is a chance to explore this full spectrum of experiences in a creative way. Think about the things that make you happy *and* the things that might bring on negative feelings. Then, use your art supplies to visually represent both sides. This can be a powerful way to gain a deeper understanding of your emotions and how they influence your life.

Steps:
1. Spend about 10 minutes perusing magazines or images from the internet for an image you love and one thing you hate.
2. Print or cut out the image you love.
3. Print or cut out the image you hate.
4. Glue both images in the journal to make a collage.
5. Change and manipulate the images by adding color and words.
6. Add more details with drawing materials.

Questions for Discussion:
1. In the image, which takes up more space—love or hate?
2. What is something you love in your life?
3. What is something you don't like in your life?
4. How can you learn to accept the situation?

Scan for video

7-6 Fork in the Road Drawing

Benefit: Increases problem-solving skills

Exercise Time: 45 minutes

Ages: Elementary 5+, middle, and high school

Materials:
- Art journal
- Assorted drawing materials (markers, oil crayons, colored pencils)

Explanation:
Making difficult decisions can be a challenge. This exercise can help you make a good decision. Imagine yourself on a journey, and you come to a fork in the road, with two paths ahead of you. Each path represents a different decision you're facing. Draw out each path, and use vivid colors and lines to depict the potential emotions you might experience along the way. For example, a bright-yellow path might symbolize excitement, while a winding path with darker colors could represent uncertainty. By visualizing these different possibilities and their associated feelings, you can gain valuable insight and make a more-informed decision.

Steps:
1. Draw out a road that comes to a fork and becomes two separate paths.
2. Each road is a different option.
3. At the end of each path, draw out the possible outcome.
4. Now choose feelings associated with each outcome.
5. Pick a color to match that feeling.
6. Place the colors of the feeling on the paths.

Questions for Discussion:
1. Which path did you pick?
2. How will your decision affect you and those around you?

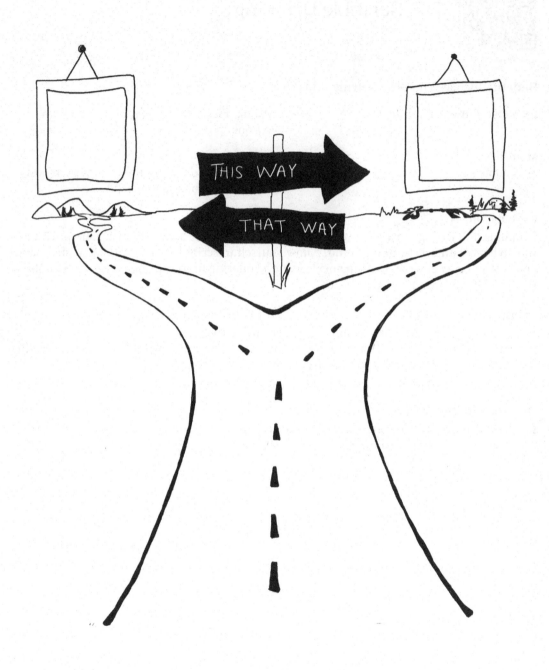

Scan for video

7-7 Scribble Drawing

Benefit: Increases problem-solving skills

Exercise Time: 30 minutes

Ages: Elementary 8+, middle, and high school

Materials:
- Art journal
- Assorted drawing media (markers, oil crayons, colored pencils)

Explanation:
Doodling and letting loose with your pen can be a surprising source of inspiration. It's a fun way to bypass an overthinking mind. Allow yourself to scribble freely. As you create, shapes and patterns may emerge, sparking new ideas and offering unique perspectives. You might be surprised by the insights that surface.

Steps:
1. Give yourself 30 seconds to a minute to draw out a scribble.
2. After drawing the scribble, take a look at the lines from different angles (turn the drawing around), let your imagination run free, and find an image.
3. Develop the image by adding more details and colors.

Questions for Discussion:
1. What can you tell me about the scribble drawing?
2. Is the object you created important to you in some way?

Scan for video

7-8 Building Bridges Drawing

Benefit: Improves problem-solving and coping skills

Exercise Time: 45 minutes

Ages: Elementary 8+, middle, and high school

Materials:
- Art journal
- Assorted drawing media (markers, oil crayons, colored pencils)

Explanation:
Imagine a problem as a wide river blocking your path to your goals. In this exercise, we'll build a bridge to cross that river, a roadmap for reaching the other side. Just like a real bridge creates the most direct path between two points, your problem-solving bridge will visualize your destination, the obstacles you'll encounter along the way, and how you'll navigate them to reach your goals.

Steps:
1. Think of a goal you want to achieve.
2. Draw out two landmasses—one representing where you are now and the other landmass a goal to achieve.
3. Draw out the bridge (e.g., wood, metal, rope).
4. Draw out any obstacles underneath the bridge that represent the challenges that would stop you from reaching the goal.
5. Color in the drawing.

Questions for Discussion:
1. Where are you on this bridge?
2. Tell me more about the obstacles.
3. Do you need support along the way?

Scan for video

7-9 Tend to Your Garden Painting

Benefit: Identifies goals and increases creative expression

Exercise Time: 45 minutes   **Ages:** Middle and high school

Materials:
- Art journal
- Assorted drawing media (markers, oil crayons, colored pencils)
- Watercolor set
- Brushes
- Water container

Explanation:
While scrolling through social media might be tempting, it can leave us feeling down. Seeing curated snapshots of others' lives can make it seem like everyone else is happier and more successful. But what if we flipped the script? Imagine your own goals and dreams as a beautiful garden. By investing time and effort in nurturing your own ideas (watering them with attention) and putting in the hard work (doing well in school, playing sports with friends, reading books, learning about new interests), you can cultivate a life that thrives and brings you genuine happiness. Tending to your own garden, rather than comparing it to someone else's, is the key to cultivating your own sense of fulfillment.

Steps:
1. Draw goals and desires as seeds in the ground.
2. Identify strengths, and represent them as trees, flowers, or vegetables in the garden.
3. Add yourself to the garden.
4. Draw out negative thoughts as weeds.
5. Fill in the background with watercolor paint.

Questions for Discussion:
1. How will you schedule more time to nurture your goals?
2. Do you need help or support along the way?

Scan for video

7-10 Treasure Island Painting

Benefit: Identifies goals and improves problem solving

Exercise Time: 45 minutes

Ages: Middle and high school

Materials:
- Art journal
- Assorted drawing media (markers, oil crayons, colored pencils)
- Watercolor set
- Brushes
- Water container

Explanation:
You hold within yourself a treasure more valuable than any gold—the power to achieve your dreams. Forget gold and jewels—this treasure map is all about you! Your true treasure lies within, in the form of peace and a calm mind. Unlike any pirate map, on this adventure, the "X" marks the spot where you want to feel your most centered and serene. The journey to this inner treasure won't always be smooth sailing. We'll map out the distractions, represented by big emotions and obstacles, like stormy seas, that you might face along the way. But fear not, with this map as your guide, you'll be well on your way to inner harmony.

Steps:
1. Draw out a beautiful island.
2. Draw out your ship approaching the island.
3. Draw out a path on the island to the secret treasure.
4. Draw the obstacles keeping you from reaching the treasure. Obstacles represent feelings that are stopping a peaceful mind (distraction, loneliness, fear).
5. Use symbolism that represents the blocks on the island (volcano, bridges, ships, sharks, etc.).
6. Fill in the background with watercolor paint.

Questions for Discussion:
1. How will you manage the distractions?
2. Do you need help or support along the way?

Chapter 8

Building Relationships

*S**trong friendships are essential building blocks** for a happy and healthy life. While friends offer a listening ear for our thoughts and ideas, their true value shines during difficult moments. Friends act as a support system, cheering us up when we're down and offering a shoulder to lean on. Sharing fun and laughter strengthens the bond and creates cherished memories. Relationships are the foundation of our well-being, providing guidance and support through life's challenges, helping us heal and grow. By nurturing these connections, we invest in our own happiness and resilience.

Scan for video

8-1 Lucky Draw Mixed Media

Benefit: Improves group communication and connection

Exercise Time: 45 minutes   **Ages:** Elementary, middle, and high school

Materials:
- Art journal
- Assorted drawing material (markers, oil crayons, colored pencils)
- Acrylic paints
- Container for ideas (bowl or jar with lid)

Explanation:

Get your friends together for an afternoon of artistic exploration. Here's the idea: Beforehand, everyone writes down a fun and surprising prompt—it could be anything that sparks inspiration, like "draw a character from a movie or video game" or "make a drawing based on your favorite song." Fold the prompts into little surprises, and toss them all in a bowl. Then, the real fun begins! Each person picks a prompt at random, so you have no idea what artistic adventure awaits. This is a fantastic way to spark new ideas, challenge yourselves creatively, and see where your imagination takes you. It's perfect for a group, so grab your friends, get ready to laugh, and unleash your inner artist.

Steps:
1. Gather your friends.
2. Each person writes out several creative ideas on paper (draw a magical castle, a robot, fast car, etc.).
3. Fold paper.
4. Place in a bowl.
5. One person chooses an activity from bowl for all to draw.
6. Each person creates their own response to the prompt.
7. Share your ideas with each other.

Questions for Discussion:
1. What was your favorite art prompt?
2. Are there any other ideas you would like to add to the bowl for next time?

Scan for video

8-2 Scribble Chase Drawing

Benefit: Increases communication and connection

Exercise Time: 45 minutes   **Ages:** Elementary, middle, and high school

Materials:
- Large butcher paper or art journal
- Assorted drawing media (markers, oil crayons, colored pencils)

Explanation:
Scribble Chase is a fantastic warm-up activity that gets everyone engaged and encourages collaboration. It's a great way to loosen up, spark creativity, and connect with others through the shared experience of creating something together. It's perfect for all skill levels, so grab your pencils and get ready to chase some artistic inspiration.

Steps:
1. Each person picks a color.
2. One person is the leader and starts the scribble, while the other person follows their lead.
3. Now switch; let the other person take the lead.
4. Just for fun, look at the drawing from different perspectives, turn the image upside down.
5. Look for an image in the drawing.
6. Bring the image out by adding more lines and colors.

Questions for Discussion:
1. How did it feel to be the leader?
2. How did it feel to be led?

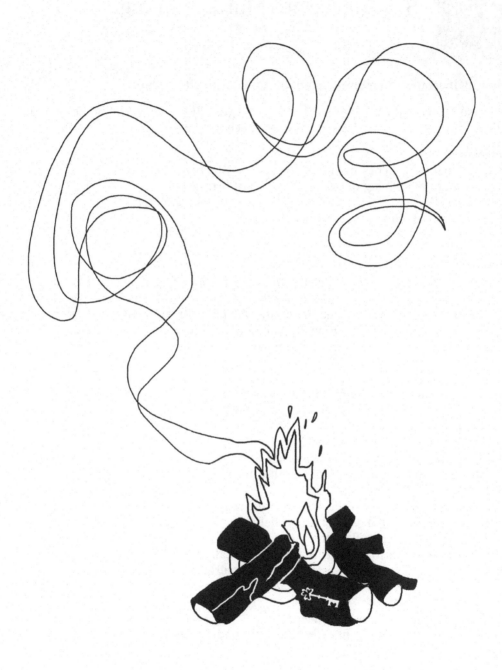

Scan for video

8-3 Marvelous Mural Painting

Benefit: Increases community, communication, and self-esteem

Exercise Time: A day to a few weeks

Ages: Elementary 5+, middle, and high school

Materials:
- Art journal for sketches and ideas
- Chalk for tracing image on wall
- Projector
- Outside paint (paint samples from paint store)
- Butcher paper
- Brushes
- Water container

Explanation:

Murals are vibrant testaments to community spirit. They bring people together in a powerful way, allowing everyone to contribute and feel a sense of accomplishment. Whether you're a seasoned artist or just starting out, there's always a place for you in the mural-making process. The key lies in thorough preparation. By planning the design, gathering materials, and working collaboratively, everyone can leave their mark and contribute to a beautiful piece of public art.

Steps:
1. Get permission from administration to paint on a school wall or community wall.
2. Pick a theme for murals (e.g., school name, logo, animals).
3. Brainstorm ideas.
4. Go online for reference material.
5. Create sketches for mural in art journal.
6. Choose colors and buy paint (use small paint samples—they go a long way).
7. Take a photo of final design.
8. Use a projector to project the design on the wall.
9. Trace image projected on wall using chalk.
10. Place butcher paper on floor to protect it from paint drips.
11. Assign individuals to paint sections of the mural.
12. Make your way, section by section, until the mural is complete.

Questions for Discussion:
1. How does this mural make you feel?
2. What other ideas do you have for future public art projects (paint benches, walls, stools)?

Scan for video

8-4 Positive Posters Painting

Benefit: Increases community, communication, and self-esteem

Exercise Time: 45 minutes

Ages: Elementary 5+, middle, and high school

Materials:
- Art journal
- Poster board
- Markers
- Pencils
- Acrylic paint

Explanation:

Have you ever felt like spreading kindness and want to make a positive impact at your school? Kindness can be as simple as a friendly "Hello" or picking up litter after lunch. Remember, even small actions can have a big impact.

This art exercise is all about creating messages that uplift and inspire others. Think about something positive you want to share with the world. Maybe it's a reminder to smile, a message of encouragement, or a call to action for a cause you care about. Get creative, and use your artwork to spread your message.

Steps:
1. Get permission from administration to hang posters on school walls.
2. Brainstorm ideas in the art journal.
3. Choose the poster's message.
4. Draw out the message in block letters with pencil.
5. Color in with markers or paint
6. Hang up in designated areas.

Question for Discussion:
1. Did you get any feedback from the community?
2. How does it feel to make a ripple effect of positivity in the world?

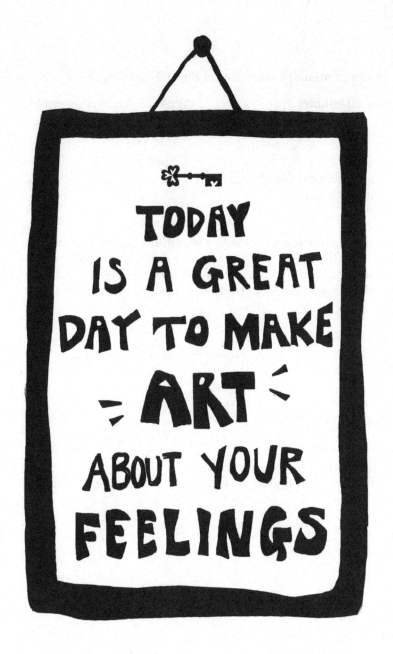

Scan for video

8-5 Round Robin Drawing

Benefit: Increases community, communication, and social skills

Exercise Time: 30 minutes

Ages: Elementary 5+, middle, and high school

Materials:
- Art journal
- Assorted drawing media (markers, oil crayons, colored pencils)
- Timer

Explanation:
Ever feel like taking a creative journey with a friend? Round Robin drawing is a fantastic way to collaborate with a friend. It's where you start a drawing, pass it to someone else, and see what they add on. Take turns building on each others' ideas for at least three minutes. You'll be amazed at how a simple sketch can transform into a unique and collaborative masterpiece.

Steps:
1. Create a drawing for three minutes.
2. Once the timer rings, give the drawing to the person to the right.
3. Set the timer for three minutes.
4. Add, change, and color image.
5. Once the timer goes off, give the journal back to its owner.
6. Set the timer again to add more to the image.

Questions for Discussion:
1. What did you think of this experience?
2. How did you feel about this process? Did you enjoy sharing your drawing?

Scan for video

8-6 Family Tree Drawing

Benefit: Exploring family dynamics and relationships

Exercise Time: 45 minutes

Ages: Elementary 5+, middle, and high school

Materials:
- Art journal
- Assorted drawing media (markers, oil crayons, colored pencils)

Explanation:

Our families are the roots that ground us. Exploring our family history can be a powerful journey of self-discovery. By understanding our family relationships, we gain a deeper appreciation for the love and support that has been passed down through generations.

Imagine your family tree as a magnificent tapestry. Each branch represents an ancestor who has contributed to your story. You may need to research and ask a family member about your relatives. As you learn about your family's history, you gain a deeper understanding of who you are and the remarkable legacy you carry forward.

Steps:
1. Outline the shape of a tree. The branches represent your family.
2. Start with yourself and siblings on the bottom branches.
3. On the left side, draw branches, and include the name of your mother and her siblings (aunts and uncles). On the next branch up, include your grandparents on your mother's side of the family.
4. On the right side, draw branches and include the name of your father and his siblings (aunts and uncles). On the next branch up, include your grandparents on your father's side of the family.
5. Go up each branch of the tree, and include more family if you like.

Questions for Discussion:
1. Who are you closest to in your family?
2. What are your favorite activities to do with your family?

8-7 Inspiring People Drawing

Benefit: Increases self-awareness and self-esteem

Exercise Time: 45 minutes

Ages: Elementary 5+, middle, and high school

Materials:
- Art journal
- Assorted drawing media (markers, oil crayons, colored pencils)

Explanation:

The people we surround ourselves with hold immense power to shape who we become. Look no further than the inspiring heroes like family members and teachers. Consider the unwavering kindness of a family member, the relentless pursuit of a friend's passion, or the enthusiasm of a teacher who sparked your curiosity. By identifying the qualities we admire in them, we gain not only inspiration but also a guiding light to illuminate our own path. Their stories and actions serve as a constant reminder of the positive impact we can make on the world. So, take a moment to reflect on the remarkable people in your life.

Steps:
1. Take a moment to reflect on a person who has inspired you.
2. Draw out the individual in your journal.
3. Add details, words, or designs.
4. List or draw out their positive qualities. Refer to Strength List p. 194.

Questions for Discussion:
1. Who did you choose to draw?
2. What aspects do you admire in this individual and hope to embrace?

Scan for video

8-8 Boundaries for Buddies Drawing

Benefit: Develops coping skills and emotional regulation

Exercise Time: 45 minutes

Ages: Elementary 5+, middle, and high school

Materials:
- Art journal
- Assorted drawing media (markers, oil crayons, colored pencils)

Explanation:

Physical boundaries are like invisible guidelines that help us feel safe and respected in our relationships. Imagine a comfortable personal space as a bubble around you. This space represents your physical boundaries, encompassing your personal comfort level with touch and closeness.

Maintaining healthy boundaries ensures everyone's well-being. Here's how respecting physical boundaries works:
- Respecting personal space: Everyone has the right to feel comfortable. This means asking permission before touching someone, hugging, or invading their personal space.
- Communicating your needs: Open communication is key. If you feel uncomfortable with someone being too close, politely, but firmly, let them know.

Remember, it's your right to set boundaries and have them respected.

Steps:
1. Draw a figure (refer to how to draw a body, p.66).
2. Draw a personal bubble to represent boundaries.
3. Decorate and design it.

Questions for Discussion:
1. Was there a time when your personal space was invaded?
2. How did you respond?
3. What would you say to someone who invades your personal space without permission?

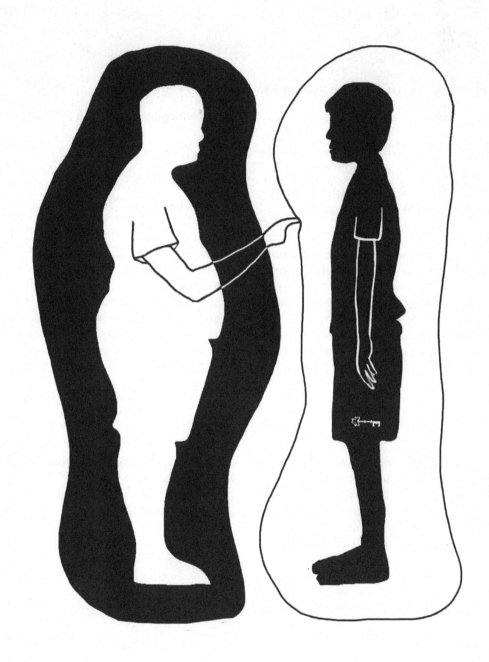

Scan for video

8-9 Emotional Wall for Protection Painting

Benefit: Develops coping skills and emotional regulation

Exercise Time: 45 minutes

Ages: elementary 5+, middle, and high school

Materials:
- Art journal
- Assorted drawing media (markers, oil crayons, colored pencils)
- Watercolor set
- Brushes
- Water container

Explanation:

Emotional boundaries protect and support healthy relationships. Imagine our emotions as a beautiful garden we have carefully nurtured. Emotional boundaries are like a safe fence protecting our garden. They ensure that our feelings are respected and valued.

- **Expressing ourselves freely:** We should feel comfortable sharing our true feelings with others. If our boundaries are disrespected, we need to let the offending person(s) know.
- **Saying no:** It's okay to set boundaries and decline requests that make us uncomfortable.
- **Protecting ourselves from negativity:** We have the right to remove ourselves from situations that drain our energy or make us feel sad. This applies to both in-person and online interactions.

Remember, we are in control of our emotions, and it's okay to speak up when our boundaries are not respected.

Steps:

1. Think of a time your emotional boundaries were not respected (e.g., someone called you a name or was rude to you).
2. Draw yourself on the page.
3. Draw out a barrier to protect your emotions (e.g., a fence or wall)
4. Add things or objects you would like inside the safe space.
5. Use watercolor to paint in the drawing.

Question for Discussion:

1. Has anyone recently disrespected your boundaries?
2. Describe how to respond if someone disrepects emotional boundaries.

Scan for video

8-10 Respecting Belongings Drawing

Benefit: Develops coping skills and emotional regulation

Exercise Time: 45 minutes

Ages: Elementary 5+, middle, and high school

Materials:
- ❧ Art journal
- ❧ Assorted drawing media (markers, oil crayons, colored pencils)

Explanation:
Everyone deserves to have their belongings treated with respect. We determine the limits on what we would like to share with others.
- Respecting personal items: Imagine our belongings having a personal "respect zone" around them. This means people need to ask permission before borrowing something and always return it on time.
- Keeping things private: Just like having a private space in our room, our belongings deserve privacy, too.

By following these simple guidelines, we can show respect for ourselves and others.

Steps:
1. Draw out items that you would like to keep for yourself on the left side of the journal.
2. Draw out items that you are willing to share with others on the right side of the journal.

Questions for Discussion:
1. How would you feel if someone disrespected your personal belongings?
2. What is a respectful way to respond to someone who disrespected your belongings?
3. Have you ever disrespected someone's belongings?

Scan for video

8-11 Stand Up to a Bully Drawing

Benefit: Builds confidence and self-advocacy skills

Exercise Time: 45 minutes

Ages: Elementary 5+, middle, and high school

Materials:
- Art journal
- Assorted drawing media (markers, oil crayons, colored pencils)

Explanation:
Sometimes, disagreements or conflicts arise between people. It's important to remember that everyone deserves to feel safe and respected. If you ever experience someone repeatedly trying to hurt you, embarrass you, threaten you, or force you into an unsafe situation, it's important to know that this behavior is called "bullying."

Remember, you are not alone. There are many people who care about you and want to help. If you are ever feeling unsafe or uncomfortable, you can always reach out to a trusted adult, such as a teacher, counselor, parent, or family member.

Steps:
1. Draw out an incident of someone being bullied.
2. Draw out a way to respond to the situation. Consider these suggestions:
   - **Stand Up for Yourself**: You need to stand up for yourself and say "No."
   - **Body Language:** When it comes to responding in an assertive way to a bully, you want to make sure that they understand how serious you are through your body language. Stand tall and confident.
   - **Tone of Voice:** While words and body language are extremely important when responding to a bully, so is your delivery and tone of voice. You want to deliver your message in a calm, strong, and confident voice.
   - **Tell a Friend, Loved One or Someone You Trust:** Don't keep this a secret. Let someone know what is going on, and ask for support. That person may be able not only to comfort you but also assist you on taking the next step.

Questions for Discussion:
1. Was the incident online or in person?
2. Was there more than one person involved?
3. Is it currently happening?
4. Who is the person that you would tell about this occurrence?

Scan for video

8-12 Kindness Stones Sculptures

Benefit: Connecting with community

Exercise Time: 45 minutes

Ages: Elementary 5+, middle, and high school

Materials:
- Smooth stones
- Paint markers
- Gesso

Explanation:

Imagine spreading tiny bursts of kindness throughout your community. Kindness stones are a fun and creative way to do just that. Here's the idea:
- Get creative: Paint rocks, pebbles, or any smooth surface with uplifting messages, words of encouragement, or even inspirational quotes.
- Spread the joy: Place the Kindness Stones around your community for others to discover.
- Gift them to friends: Surprise a friend with a personalized Kindness Stone, spreading a little happiness their way.
- Create a Kindness Corner: Gather your creations, and display them in a designated space at school, like a reading nook or a bulletin board.

Kindness Stones are a reminder that even small acts of kindness can make a big difference. By leaving these positive messages around, you can brighten someone's day and inspire others to do the same!

Steps:
1. Gather smooth stones (purchase or find them outside).
2. Gesso to prep stones.
3. Let dry.
4. Use paint markers to design stones.
5. Add a word or positive statement on the stone.

Questions for Discussion:
1. What did you choose to write on the stone?
2. Is there a stone you'd like to keep for yourself?
3. Where would you like to place the stones?

Scan for video

8-13 Pieces of a Pie Mandala Painting

Benefit: Creating community and a sense of belonging

Exercise Time: 45 minutes

Ages: Elementary 5+, middle, and high school

Materials:
- Large butcher paper
- Assorted drawing media (markers, oil crayons, colored pencils)
- Acrylic paint
- Brushes
- Water container

Explanation:

Mandalas are a geometric drawings used for relaxation and focus. Working in a group, each person will get a chance to design their own section of the mandala, incorporating personal style and creativity. Once everyone has completed their art, the individual sections will be assembled to form a stunning collaborative mandala. Before you begin working, take some deep breaths, and let your mind wander. Making a mandala involves repetitive motions that are very calming and promote a sense of peace and well-being.

Steps:
1. Draw out large circle on butcher paper.
2. Draw out pie slices (enough for each person in the group).
3. Each person gets a piece of the pie to decorate.
4. Pick a theme for the mandala, or have everyone trace their hand.
5. Add your own, personal design and color.
6. Hang mandala in community area for everyone to appreciate.

Questions for Discussion:
1. What feeling came up for you while you were creating your mandala?
2. Where would you like to hang the collaborative masterpiece?

Scan for video

8-14 Favorite Friend Selfie Mixed Media Collage

Benefit: Builds relationships and self-awareness

Exercise Time: 45 minutes   **Ages:** Elementary, middle, and high school

Materials:
- Art journal
- Stickers
- Assorted drawing media (markers, oil crayons, colored pencils)
- Selfie picture of you and a friend printed

Explanation:
Friends are like the vibrant flowers that bloom in our garden of life. They add beauty, joy, and fragrance to our world. Hold onto these special moments with your friend by taking a picture together. Print it out, and decorate it with things that symbolize the fun activities you enjoy doing together. It'll be a wonderful reminder of your cherished friendship.

Steps:
1. Take a picture of your and your friend.
2. Cut out the background.
3. Glue image to the art journal.
4. Add details of favorite activities and memories.

Questions for Discussion:
1. What are fun things you like to do with your friend?
2. What is your favorite memory of you and your friend together?

Scan for video

8-15 Favorite Friend Feltie Plushie

Benefit: Increases empathy and builds relationships

Exercise Time: 2 sessions of 45 minutes each **Ages:** Elementary 5+, middle school

Materials:
- Felt
- Hot glue (or needle and thread)
- Polyester filling
- Scissors
- Paper
- Art journal

Explanation:
Imagine creating a little buddy, a plushie you can keep close. Think about the characteristics you admire in your friends—kindness, humor, loyalty. As you design your plushie, incorporate elements that represent the qualities you admire in your friend—maybe a big smile for someone who always makes you laugh or a heart for a friend who's always supportive.

Steps:
1. Draw out a friend in the art journal.
2. List out all their best characteristics and qualities.
3. Trace out the shape onto paper to use as a template.
4. Place felt under template, and cut out.
5. Repeat the last step so that you have both a front and a back of the friend.
6. Hot-glue edges on the inside, or sew together pieces.
7. Leave space to fill with stuffing.
8. Add details with felt, and attach (eyes, ears, clothing, etc.)

Questions for Discussion:
1. What is your plushie's name?
2. Will you keep the plushie or give it to a friend?

Strength List

Adaptable

Ambitious

Articulate

Awesome

Bold

Calm

Candid

Charismatic

Clearheaded

Communicative

Competitive

Considerate

Cooperative

Courageous

Creative

Curious

Decisive

Dedicated

Determined

Devoted

Diligent

Efficient

Emotional Intelligence

Empathetic

Enthusiastic

Experienced

Flexible

Focused

Forthright

Gifted

Hard-working

Helpful

Honest

Humble

Humor

Imaginative

Independent

Innovative

Insightful

Intuitive

Inventive

Involved

Kind

Lovable

Mature

Methodical

Meticulous

Motivated

Natural Leader

Neat

Objective

Open-minded

Organized

Outspoken

Passionate

Patient

Perceptive

Persuasive

Polite

Positive

Practical

Problem-solver

Prudent

Punctual

Realistic

Reliable

Resourceful

Respectful

Responsible

Seasoned

Self-confident

Self-directed

Self-disciplined

Sensible

Sincere

Sociable

Systematic

Team Player

Thorough

Thoughtful

Trustworthy

Unique

Versatile

Well-rounded

Willing

Feeling List

Angry	Confused	Happy	Sad
Cross	Doubtful	Pleased	Upset
Irritated	Uncertain	Delighted	Hurt
Annoyed	Indecisive	Joyful	Crushed
Displeased	Hesitant	Cheerful	Down
Enraged	Baffled	Content	Miserable
Furious	Perplexed	Glad	Unhappy
Hateful	Bewildered	Enthusiastic	Blue
Hostile	Chaotic	Jolly	Gloomy

Calm	Scared	Loved	Tired
Relaxed	Afraid	Beloved	Stressed
Still	Terrified	Cherished	Drained
Quiet	Fearful	Admired	Exhausted
Peaceful	Anxious	Supported	Fatigued
Restful	Nervous	Special	Disconnected
Composed	Suspicious	Valued	Empty
Tranquil	Worried	Wanted	Overworked
Serene	Alarmed	Adored	Burned Out

I hope you enjoyed this book. Would you do me a favor?

Like all authors, I rely on online reviews to encourage future sales.

Your opinion is invaluable. Would you take a few moments now to share your assessment of my book at the review site of your choice?

Your opinion will help the book marketplace
become more transparent and useful to all.

Thank you very much!

You are welcome to get your art kit and more fun tools at
www.leahguzmanstudio.com

Be sure to post your art on our private Facebook group
Creative Soul Online Retreat.

Here are some additional resources that can help:

- The National Bullying Prevention Center:
  https://www.pacer.org/bullying/

- StopBullying.gov:
  https://www.stopbullying.gov/

- The Trevor Project (for LGBTQ youth):
  https://www.thetrevorproject.org/

- National Suicide Prevention Hotline
  https://988lifeline.org/

- American Art Therapy Association
  https://arttherapy.org/

- Book: *The Education Revolution: How to Apply Brain Science to Improve Instruction and School Climate*, by Horacio Sanchez

- Join the Creative Soul Society membership to continue a creative self-care practice https://www.leahguzmanstudio.com/creative-soul-society-membership

About the Author

*L*eah Guzman, ATR-BC, is a professional artist and board-certified art therapist. She supports creatives with healing and manifesting their desires utilizing art media through several art therapy services and coaching.

She has written several art therapy books, that are international best sellers, *Essential Art Therapy Exercises: Effective Techniques to Manage Anxiety, Depression, and PTSD, Anxiety Relief Activity Book, Art of Healing and Manifesting* and is the author of a children's book, *Rad Is Smad!*

Leah supports creatives by healing emotional wounds and transforming energy to be their most authentic self. She focuses on the Law of Attraction, spirituality, and cognitive-behavioral art therapy techniques. She also has other online courses, such as the Creative Soul Society, a monthly art-making membership group, and art-as-therapy painting classes on her website.

Leah has a consistent art-making practice. Her art is mixed-media paintings that embody high energy, richness in color, visual harmony, and beauty. She lives in Miami, Florida, with her husband, Jorge, and two beautiful children, Joaquin and Carmen. She received a Bachelor of Fine Arts degree in studio sculpture from Georgia State University and then studied painting at the San Francisco Art Institute. Later, she earned a Master's degree in Art Therapy at Florida State University and became a Board Certified Art Therapist.

"It's an honor to have supported thousands of creatives in finding more joy, wealth, and peace in their lives through my techniques."
~LEAH GUZMAN